A Million MFAs Are Not Enough

A MILLION MFAs
ARE NOT ENOUGH
Essays on Revitalizing American Poetry

Charles Harper Webb

 Red Hen Press | *Pasadena, CA*

Book layout by Selena Trager

ISBN: 978-1-59709-724-6
eISBN: 978-1-59709-513-6

The National Endowment for the Arts, the Los Angeles County Arts Commission, the Los Angeles Department of Cultural Affairs, the Dwight Stuart
Youth Fund, the Pasadena Arts & Culture Commission and the City of Pasadena Cultural Affairs Division, Sony Pictures Entertainment, and the Ahman-
son Foundation partially support Red Hen Press.

First Edition
Published by Red Hen Press
www.redhen.org

Acknowledgments

I would like to thank the editors of the following publications for first publishing these essays, sometimes in another version:

Chiron Review: "Five Stand Up Poets"; *ELF: Eclectic Literary Forum*: "Depression and American Poetry: A Psychotherapeutic Approach"; *Humor*: "A Defense of Humor in Poetry" (as "Say There Was"); *New York Quarterly*: "In Defense of Clarity"; *Poetry Flash*: "Where I Stand"; *Salt Hill*: "How I Met the Prose Poem, and What Ensued"; *The Cortland Review*: "The Pleasure of Their Company: Voice and Poetry"; *The MacGuffin*: "The Myth of Maturity"; *The Writer's Chronicle*: "Apples and Orangutans: Competing Values in Contemporary Poetry," "Back to the Narrative: Breathing New Life into a Tired Form," "How Do They Do It?: The Powerful Poems of Dorianne Laux and B. H. Fairchild," "The Limits of Indeterminacy: A Defense of Less Difficult Poetry," "The Poem as Fitness Display," and "The Quick and the Dead: An Energy Crisis in Poetry."

Contents

A Million MFAs Are Not Enough

Foreword

Back in the Pleistocene, when I made my living playing rock-and-roll, I thought that poetry could and should be as popular as Led Zeppelin. I proclaimed with confidence that any reader able to understand and enjoy *Time* magazine should be able to understand and enjoy at least some contemporary poetry.

Years of teaching have taught me that, for most readers, any poem worthy of the name will be more challenging than *Time*. I now accept that Billy Collins, Mary Oliver, and Sharon Olds combined will never approach the popularity of Lil Wayne or Justin Bieber. Still, I believe that, with respect to audience *and* artistry, poetry has shot itself in many portions of its anatomy, and keeps blasting. The fact that vast numbers of poems are published every year, and a large number of creative writing students and graduates combine to read a few of them, does not mean that poetry is on the right track. A million MFAs are not enough to make poetry count in the culture-at-large.

From the publication of "Five Stand Up Poets" in 1989 until now, I've tried, in poems and essays, to counter the forces that have consigned the erstwhile Queen of the Arts to the tiny corner of the cultural basement where she languishes today. Why don't more Americans like poetry? Why do so many fear and/or ignore it? Why do the majority of prestigiously published, well-reviewed books of contemporary poems seem to me dull as tax code, and almost as punishing? What, if anything, might change the situation? Does it need changing? What makes a poem good? What makes one interesting? Are they the same things? What are those things?

The essays in this book wrestle with these and other questions, defining problems and suggesting solutions. Many of the essays take the form of craft lectures. Others are more personal. All are, I hope, opinionated but not unreasonable.

I favor poems that speak, at least potentially, to a readership beyond the specialist. I believe that meaning exists, and expect poems to communicate it, even though "it" may be hard to paraphrase. I resent poems that, like little Enigma codes, require deciphering. I don't like poets to obfuscate—especially when what they've hidden proves to be fool's gold. I like poems that give pleasure and are understandable the first time through, but reward rereading with increased pleasure, depth, and resonance. Such poems enlighten as they entertain.

I hope that these essays will do that too.

Apples and Orangutans:
Competing Values in Contemporary Poetry

The Elizabethan poet's situation was, I'm sure, more complicated than it seems, looked back on from the twenty-first century. I can imagine feuds: enjambed versus end-stopped lines, traditional versus contemporary diction, suitable and unsuitable subjects for poetry. Still, poets had many areas of agreement: accepted rules of syntax, diction, coherence, as well as the need for rhyme and/or meter. Boundaries might be stretched, but were rarely breached by serious practitioners of the art. Comparing poems might not always have been apples to apples, or even crabapples to pippins, but it was not apples to landfills, or dirt-bikes, or orangutans, as it often is today.

Poetry has become such a wide open field, such an anything-goes battle zone, that it's hard to find areas of universal tolerance, much less agreement. Neo-beat, meat, academic, street, slam, formalist, L=A=N=G=U=A=G=E, experimental, elliptical, stand up, Stoogist, imagist, deep imagist, avant-garde, prose, post-structuralist, modern, High Modern, post-modern, and post-post-modern are just a few of the adjectives applied to poets as diverse as Richard Wilbur, Charles Bukowski, John Ashbery, Ron Silliman, Michael McClure, Rita Dove, James Tate, Patty Seyburn, Mark Strand, Lyn Hejinian, Jorie Graham, Sharon Olds, Edward Hirsch, Denise Duhamel, Elaine Equi, Charles Bernstein, Patricia Smith, Billy Collins, Alicia Ostriker, Gary Snyder, Ed Ochester, Ray Gonzalez, Wanda Coleman, Richard Garcia, Gerald Locklin, David St. John, Sparrow, Ron Koertge, Aram Saroyan, Russell Edson, and Brenda Hillman.

Since poetry in the United States rarely posts big sales, and is infrequently reviewed, once books are published, the marketplace and critics do little winnowing. With no natural selection operating, any type of poem, no matter how ill-suited for life, can survive, and even prosper if it finds a few supporters—especially loud ones emanating from universities.

The situation gives poets enormous freedom, but also creates enormous frustration and befuddlement. It offers poetry readers and prospective readers dizzying choices, but can give them fits. Poetry is already viewed by the general public as a field likely to make those foolish enough to enter feel more foolish still. Though contemporary poetry offers something for virtually everyone, the sheer amount of published work makes it hard for the reader—especially the neophyte—to find books to his/her own taste.

As for critical assessment of poetry—how does one competently assess something when there is no agreement what that thing should be?

If assessment is by committee, decisions normally flow toward a middle ground, excluding the unusual (hence, the truly innovative), and the great. Assessment by one person is necessarily subjective. Unlike the hundred-meter dash, where the fastest time wins, contemporary poetry can offer few, if any, objective criteria for winning. A writer of first-rate formal verse may be the very thing a lover of experimental verse finds most unworthy, and vice versa.

Yet critics often write as if their opinions must necessarily be shared by all right-thinking people. Poets often think of those in other aesthetic camps as deluded, foolish, benighted, short-sighted, stupid, dull, insensitive, and not much short of depraved.

I've done my share of fulminating against values that I believe to foster bad writing, alienate readers, and doom poetry to cultural insignificance. I'm convinced my positions are right. I'm also convinced that differences in aesthetics—i.e., taste—arise, in the main, not from reasoned judgment, but from temperament. Some differences are biological: inborn attitudes and tendencies almost impossible to change. Most of the rest are psychological—learned at an early age, and highly resistant to change. Relatively few, I believe, are products of conscious choice. People react, then rationalize their reactions.

I often hear that poets should support each other because, "We're all, first and foremost, poets." I applaud any idea that encourages people to be kind to each other. Still it should be noted that poets in the United States today may have no more in common than Montana fly fishermen have with Antarctic gillnetters. What is praised in one quarter is sure to be vilified in another, and its opposite praised. People come to poetry wanting, needing, demanding different and frequently incompatible things.

Below are a number of such "things," along with a brief explanation of each. Even within these divisions, though, there are disagreements, and many possible subdivisions. I offer the following, not to limit the diversity, not to solve the problem (if it is a problem), not to bring one group or another to its senses, but merely to highlight, and marvel at, some of the competing values that exist among poets and/or readers of poetry in the United States today.

1. Natural language

Poetry should be written in straightforward language, clearly and concisely saying what it means. It should be written in the language people actually use, unencumbered by obscure allusions or references. Nothing should be written in a poem that a person could not conceivably say in a conversation.

   1A. Free form. Rhyme and meter are unnatural, and/or oppressive, and/or inhibiting, and/or elitist, and/or not reflective of modern American life. The best contemporary poetry is necessarily free verse, or possibly prose poetry, which breaks down the artificial division between poetry and prose. Some proponents of free verse give great weight to effective use of line breaks; others, to the poem's appearance on the page.

   1B. A plain style. Poetry should eschew all preciousness. It should strip away poeticisms and verbal flourishes. It should be simple and direct, with no pyrotechnics, and no pretension. Understatement is a virtue. Metaphor should be minimized; it smacks of falseness, and impedes the forward movement of the poem.

2. Special language

Poetry is not everyday speech, but language set apart. This set-apartness may be expressed through poetic devices such as rhyme, meter, and erudite allusions, or by using language in non-standard ways. Poetry should allow readers to savor elevated diction, or perhaps disjunctive sentences and indeterminate syntax. Or natural language should be crafted so as to make it special.

   2A. Figures of speech. The essence of poetry is metaphor. Through this imaginative linking of unlike things, poetry can approach the ineffable.

2B. Music. The sound of poetry is related to, but more important than, whatever "sense" the poem contains. Proponents may say, "I don't know what it means, but it sounds great." Readers may approach the ecstatic through sound.

2C. Flash and flair. Poetry is language-intoxication. A poem is the perfect place to display verbal panache and excess in the manner of Shakespeare. Overstatement can be a virtue.

2D. Fixed form. Poetry at its best makes use of rhyme and/or meter. Anything less is "playing tennis without a net."

3. Difficulty

Since poetry is language working at its highest potential, it is necessarily (and delightfully) challenging. A good poem requires many readings, and considerable (often professional) interpretation. Easy poetry is inferior poetry.

4. Clarity

The greatest writing of the past has been clear, and contemporary writing should be the same. Obscurity means bad writing. Ambiguity may be good, but only if multiple meanings do not cancel out or deconstruct each other.

4A. Accessibility. Poetry should be reader-friendly, or in the words of Billy Collins, "hospitable." It should be available to a large audience and, at least on a surface level, require little or no interpretation.

4B. A determinable meaning. A good poem accurately conveys the author's meaning to the reader. It is a successful act of interpersonal communication.

5. Indeterminacy

All claims to insight into the human mind are suspect, as is the concept of "truth." By refusing to be freighted with or trapped inside a given "meaning," poetry best illuminates the so-called "human condition," which is also indeterminate. Meaning is impossible, or at least undecidable, since for any statement, there is a multiplicity of possible, often contradictory, meanings. Ambiguity is unavoidable, multiple meanings serving to contradict, cancel out, and deconstruct each other.

6. Opacity
Clarity traps the reader in stale, enervated, writer-directed ideas and perception. Opaque elements in a poem force the reader to participate actively in the creation of meaning.

7. Mystery
Poetry should not put all its cards on the table. Clarity is a virtue of prose, if it is a virtue at all. Poetry is beyond logic. Its realm is the ineffable, which is not reachable via "normal" linguistic paths. Ambiguity may be savored for its own sake.

8. A fresh look at life
Poetry refreshes the world, making the audience see with "new eyes." This effect (literary code-name: defamiliarization) may be achieved through the devices of traditional prosody and/or by techniques of the avant-garde. For a poem to succeed, it must transform the everyday, taken-for-granted world into something new, interesting, and strange.

9. Epiphany
Poems should be about large, life-changing events and/or revelations.

10. Memorable moments
Poems should be like snapshots: small but potent slices of real and/or imaginative life. They concretize and commemorate experiences that would otherwise be lost.

11. Puzzles to solve and codes to break
One of the joys of poetry is the chance to test one's wits against the text. What are the symbols, and how are they used? What are the patterns of imagery, and why do they exist? What meanings lurk under the surface of the poem?

11A. Verbal play. Poetry is language working at its highest potential; therefore, the more meaning that can be layered into it via puns, homonyms, acrostics, and other games and tricks, the better.

12. Seriousness

Although it is sometimes argued that humor and even outright silliness may be used for serious artistic purposes, readers must save their highest (and perhaps their sole) regard for works of high and sober seriousness.

13. Wit and humor

These qualities may be expressed in forms ranging from academic quips to X-rated fantasies to slapstick, each style having its critics, and its fans. Though few poets or critics would exclude wit and humor from poetry, the value ascribed to it ranges from very high to negligible.

13A. Ridiculousness. All human endeavor is absurd, and poetry is especially so. This is best expressed by poetry that parodies Poetry with such lines as "I am in a butt."[1]

14. Sincerity

Aphorisms abound concerning the relation (frequently inverse) of sincerity to good poetry. Yet the quality is highly prized in many quarters. Its perceived lack may disqualify a poem from consideration as serious art.

15. Irony

This quality, which can include self-mockery, is fundamental to post-modernism, which takes as given that humankind has lost its position at the center of the universe, and been relegated to an insignificant planet orbiting a minor star. David Lehman calls irony ". . . the attitude of mind best suited to the presentation of an internal conflict . . . [and] intense ambivalence. Irony also suggests a certain kind of literary structure in which oppositions coexist and paradoxes can prevail."[2] Post-modern irony is often of the scornful kind.

16. A chance to feel intelligent

Because good poetry conveys much information in relatively few words, even the most transparent verse requires more brainpower, and necessitates more mental leaps, than an equal amount of prose. The self-esteem

---

1 Gabriel Gudding, "Statement," in *A Defense of Poetry* (Pittsburgh: University of Pittsburgh Press, 2002): 83.
2 David Lehman, "Twenty Questions," interview by Nin Andrews, in *The Line Forms Here* (Ann Arbor: University of Michigan Press, 1992): 240.

derived from proving oneself up to the task is one of the least frequently acknowledged benefits of reading poems.

17. A chance to co-create the poem
Poems should allow the reader's mind to go wherever it is moved to go, without any struggling toward a "correct" interpretation. A good poem expects intense reader engagement in the creative process, and functions mainly as an aide to the reader's imagination. There should be no "privileging" of author over reader. Author-imposed meanings are oppressive.

18. A chance to willingly suspend disbelief
Good poetry induces a waking dream. Like a surfer who yields most of his power of movement to a wave, readers place themselves in the poet's hands, hoping to be taken somewhere appealing. All hypnosis is self-hypnosis.

19. Vivid imagery
Poetry works through T. S. Eliot's "objective correlative"—emotion evoked in the brain through imagery.

20. Emotional power
The heart of poetry is emotion, and poetry should have "heart." It should pack an emotional wallop. Emphasis on ideas may be seen as "heady," inimical to poetry.

21. Intellectual power
Poetry should be unabashedly intellectual, full of ideas—philosophical, political, scientific (or whatever a given reader enjoys). Strong emotions may be seen as irrelevant, soft-headed, or worst or all, sentimental. Poetry, as Eliot claimed, is an *escape* from emotion.

22. No ideas but in things
Poetry is not the place to examine intellectual issues. If they are explored, they should be embodied in concrete, non-intellectual imagery.

23. Associative leaps
Poets display their virtuosity by nimble, fluid, wild, and frequently non-linear associations. The pleasure in reading is akin to watching a trapeze artist make one dazzling jump after another.

24. Moral, mental, spiritual, psychological uplift
Poetry should be a source of inspiration and encouragement. It embodies the virtues of the culture, and helps to pass them on.

25. Art for art's sake
Art answers to no power above itself. It is not an agent of social utility, nor should it be. It constitutes its own and only justification.

26. Past literary glories revisited
Contemporary poetry should do what great poems of the past did. It should be in harmony with, and part of, a Great Tradition.

27. Avant-garde approach
Poetry should be in the forefront of human thought, feeling, and perception. Above all else, poems should, in Ezra Pound's words, "make it new."

28. Imagination
Though most poets and readers laud imagination, they may disagree violently as to what it is, and how it is expressed.

29. Entertainment and fun.
Some people crave these qualities in poetry; others find such considerations more appropriate for lowbrow entertainment such as movies, crime novels, or TV.

   29A. Performability. Poetry is an oral art, and the best poems work best when presented orally. Some fans of poetry don't want to read it, but to hear it at readings.

   29B. Excitement and energy. Like rock music, poetry should set the mind running and the body pulsing.

30. Relaxed contemplation
Poetry should be a kind of meditation, lowering the pulse and calming the mind.

31. Boredom
Poetry that amuses or entertains can't move readers' minds out of their cultural ruts. A poem of brilliant images and epiphanies is artificial and unnatural. Numbing repetition or befuddling non sequiturs may force the reader to enter into creative partnership with the writer, and not simply fall back into passivity.

32. Careful crafting
Poetry should be painstakingly crafted, even if the result is to seem not crafted at all.

33. Spontaneity
Poetry should be the uninhibited effusion of a moment. "First word, best word."

34. Cohesion and unity
Poems should provide flowing, fully evoked descriptions or narratives, presented with a logical progression of images and ideas. All elements should work together to create a unified experience. Ambiguity may be a good thing, but only if multiple meanings do not cancel out or deconstruct each other.

35. Fragmentation
Poems should reflect the discontinuity of human life. Logic is not to be trusted, and may be an instrument of patriarchal oppression. Real-life experience is not unified; neither should poetry be.

36. Closure
A poem's ending should be strong and decisive, with powerful resonance.

    36A. Elusive closure. A poem's ending should be less a door slamming and more a whisper. It should suggest possibilities, not state a conclusion.

37. Absence of closure
Closure is unnatural, and limits the poem. A poem's conclusion should maximize the poem's openness to interpretation.

38. Psychological insight

The ability to explore the human psyche is the great strength of literature, and therefore, of poetry. Poetry should help readers to reach a deeper understanding—psychological, intellectual, and emotional—of themselves and others.

38A. *True confessions.* Poetry should explore emotions and events that are normally kept hidden. Poetry is the place to expose one's shames, and exorcise one's demons. Readers may therefore be helped to normalize their own difficult emotions and experiences, and come to terms with their own secrets. Poems provide a kind of psychotherapy.

38B. *Impropriety.* Since standards of propriety are meant to keep unpleasant, upsetting, and potentially dangerous truths out of mind, and since good poetry tells the truth—however provisional, shaky, and subjective it may be—poetry will necessarily violate these standards. It may deal with (and even celebrate) the inglorious, ignoble, violent, illegal, and mean. It may, and perhaps should, transgress.

39. Propriety

Poetry should celebrate by example the virtues of restraint, reticence, decorum. It embodies and reinforces important cultural ideas and norms.

40. Wisdom and timeless values

Poetry should be a repository of important human truths, able to guide and help readers in their lives. Great poetry expresses, in the words of Alexander Pope, "what oft was thought but ne'er so well expressed."

41. Detachment

Poetry should aim for the objective, ego-less voice of Science. At the very least, it should avoid self-obsession, and eschew the first person "I." The author, if not stone dead, is merely the physical entity through which language makes the limited number of statements that its own structure allows. "Personality" is inimical to successful poetry.

42. A strong individual voice

Poetry is all about the human personality, as expressed and embodied in the individual manner of speaking/writing—i.e., the voice. The poet's "I"-ness should not only be explored, but also, if interesting enough, indulged. This voice may or may not be closely related (or identical) to the speaking voice of the poet. The successful poet's voice is distinct from all others. The use of the first person "I" is good. Mark Halliday describes the intention of a good poem as follows: "If I could speak to you, or if a deep part of my being could speak directly, truly, powerfully, to the center of you . . . then it would sound like this."[3]

42A. *Freshness of expression.* This quality, like imagination, is admired by most (but not all) poets, though they may fight over what the quality is, and how it should be expressed. This freshness not only gives pleasure; it renews and revitalizes the language.

43. A sense of relativism
All values are time- and culture-dependent. There is no absolute "truth." The so-called truths of our culture are oppressive lies.

44. A sense of shared experience
Poetry should give readers a feeling of commonality with other people, past and present. It should increase our sense of empathy, and help us to feel less alone.

44A. *A sense of being part of an elite.* Poetry is necessarily for the few, and therefore is esoteric. Part of the pleasure of reading poems is to savor this fact.

45. Recognition of essential aloneness
Poetry should demonstrate and embody the futility of expecting company on one's life journey. How can we know another person, when it is impossible even to pinpoint an "I"?

46. A good story
The best poetry is narrative. Poetry without a narrative element is gelded poetry.

47. Lyrical beauty
The highest form of contemporary poetry is the lyric, which does not need, and may be debased by, a narrative component.

---

3 Matthew Cooperman, "Walking and Talking: An Interview with Mark Halliday," *The Writer's Chronicle* (February 2002): 57.

48. A particular world view
Many readers reject work that embodies a worldview different from their own. To be excellent, the poem must share the reader's own outlook. (People who feel this way will most likely deny it.)

48A. Women's/racial/ethnic issues. The most interesting poetry deals with [fill in oppressed group]'s concerns, and should help to empower them. Proponents often state their views proudly and openly.

48B. White men's issues. The most interesting poetry deals with white men's concerns, and should help them to keep the power they have, and regain any power they have lost. Proponents tend to conceal their views, sometimes even from themselves.

49. Re-creation of life experience
Using imagery, sound, dramatic pacing, and other techniques of prosody, a good poem re-creates, in the reader's mind, the author's real or imagined experience. Reading poems is a way for the reader to gain vicarious life experience.

50. Creation of a new linguistic experience
Language is not life, and can't re-create it. A poem is an experience of language, which must be distorted, fragmented, or otherwise teased out of normal usage to create something new and hitherto unknown.

51. Realism
Narrative and description should be based on, and centered around, the world in which human beings live.

52. Surrealism
The dream realm of the unconscious is the proper subject of poetry. Fantastical happenings are more interesting and meaningful than the quotidian, and just as real, being a part of mental life. Poetry should express and celebrate unfettered imagination.

53. A map of awareness
Poetry is the linguistic charting of consciousness at work and play. John Ashbery employs a fluid, gliding style that seems to erase its meaning as the sentence unfolds. Lyn Hejinian uses discontinuous sentences and fragments, with much leaping about, to mirror her thought process. Denise

Duhamel uses multiple digressions. In a sense, all poetry is about writing poetry.

54. Compression
Poetry is powerful thought squeezed into a small space. It is language under pressure, as in the poems of Dickinson.

55. Rhapsodic flow
Poetry is an upswelling of life-energy—powerful, fecund, and abundant, as in the poems of Whitman. Slavish sticking to a point or theme is intrinsically unpoetic.

56. Impeded forward progress
Poetry should employ stumbling blocks—opaque language, repetitions, interruptions, even simple boredom—to keep the reader from passively succumbing to the writer's control.

57. Beauty
Poetry should be concerned with the beautiful, the fine, and the refined. Subtle, graceful, and deft, it should appeal to our higher nature.

    57A. Beauty in ugliness. Poetry should bring out the beauty in what is normally not considered beautiful.

58. Anti-Beauty
Poetry should deal with life as it is, stripped of pretense, presented in all its grit, grime, and brutality. Poems should be raw, explosive, and unpolished. The cult of beauty is outdated, exclusionary, and oppressive.

59. Disguised technique
Through skillful use of craft, poetry should create in the reader a "waking dream." The poet works very hard to make it seem as if he or she didn't work at all.

60. Laid-bare technique
Poetry should call attention to its tricks and secrets. It should not try to create a "waking dream," but should be honest about its status as a verbal artifact.

The list could go on, but I hope the point is made.

If you're a poet trying to publish your work, it's best to know what values are "out there," and which publishers share yours. There's no point in sending a perfect apple to someone who only wants to see orangutans.

If you're a baffled reader, it helps to understand that not only is most contemporary poetry bad (as most poetry in all ages has been bad), good poetry written from an aesthetic different from your own may also seem bad to you. Critics' aesthetic positions can be deduced from their writing, and factored into your assessment of their assessments.

If you're a beginning writer of poetry, it's useful, through wide reading and deep self-scrutiny, to refine your taste and clarify your personal aesthetic. What do you want your poetry, and others', to do? At all stages in a writing life, and most especially the early ones, it's best to keep an open mind. An individual's taste naturally changes over time. Lock it in, and your work may cease to grow.

If you're a veteran reader and/or writer of poetry, it's good to understand how the world of American poetry has changed in even the last twenty years. Awards and competitions—more and more the keys to status in the world of Poetry—continue to be fluky and undependable indices of excellence. Reviews and criticism are more unpredictable and frustrating than ever. Acknowledging the full range of editorial preferences may not ease the frustration, but it can lessen confusion and self-doubt when you're sure you've written well, yet get a negative response. It may help you reaffirm what you're trying to do.

American poetry in 2016 is an expanding universe, poets streaking away from one another, becoming more and more diverse. Yet at some point in the future, this expansion will certainly stop. Some writer or theorist may at this moment be creating work that will change everything, turn everything around. Then, like a collapsing universe, poets may coalesce into a state of near-unanimity, ready to heat up and explode again.

Five Stand Up Poets

On Stand Up Poetry

Since the following essay appeared in *The Chiron Review* (1989), I've written several updates, most recently in *Stand Up Poetry: An Expanded Anthology* (2002). It's now 2016. The term Stand Up Poetry has entered the national lexicon, though not always in accordance with the definition I roughed out below. Stand Up itself has been absorbed into the poetic mainstream. Billy Collins, a quintessential Stand Up poet, has shown that poetry that combines high literary quality with high entertainment value can attract a large, non-specialist audience. Yet American poetry still, for the most part, lacks the energy, the accessibility, the audacity, the fervor, ferocity, and anything-goes spirit of fun and *joie de vivre* that I celebrated in this, my first in a series of aesthetic calls-to-arms.

Five Stand Up Poets

Reams have been written on the schools and divisions of American poetry. Questions of style, philosophy, and lineage aside, though, the simple fact is that any poet in America can be lumped into one of two groups: inside or outside the Charmed Circle. Insiders publish books with major houses, win major awards, are regularly included in well-distributed magazines and anthologies, and have, therefore, the best chance to become known. Outsiders are everyone else.

The favored way to get inside nowadays is to land—usually via a creative writing program—a mentor who is already inside. Since poetry in the United States is not expected to sell or be widely read, there is no trial-by-marketplace. Reputation is the currency of modern poetry; and reputation means the approval of Insiders. They judge the contests, give the grants, edit the "best" journals, and choose the books that will be prestigiously published. The poets they select are automatically In. And they rarely select from outside the Creative Writing Club.

Undeniably, creative writing graduates write some fine poetry. But great poetry was being written long before anyone heard of an MFA. The creative writing workshop is not the only way to write good poetry, and in fact can present dangers. Poet Donald Hall decries the "interchangeable" workshop poem as "indistinguishable, undistinguished . . . identical from coast to coast."[4]

"Our time may well be characterized by more mediocrity, and less badness,"[5] Hall declares. And it is true that many Insiders, young and old, seem content with competence—afraid, one suspects, to take a chance and risk a fall from grace. They choose safe subjects, and write about them in safe ways: emotions muted, scenes and settings hazy, themes opaque. But playing it safe leads, inevitably, to dullness. And dull is what poetry can't afford to be, in these days when the *Los Angeles Times* compares poetry to an "endangered species,"[6] and even English teachers rarely read contemporary poems.

Possibly as a reaction to being ignored, some poets—not just Insiders—adopt a haughty attitude toward the idea of "audience." Poetry, they state, is necessarily an elite Art, not suited to the rabble, who prove their rabblehood by staying away.

This is a foolish and ultimately fatal affectation. Even eliminating the general public, there is a huge middle audience of educated, intelligent people who read novels, go to plays and galleries, and are generally interested in the Arts. But these people too shun poetry. Why? Because, I think, most of it doesn't speak to them.

Poetry has become the starveling of the art world, a laughingstock to be sneered at in beer commercials, because it has scorned its audience. What is needed to reach the huge, and appropriate audience of intelligent laypersons, may well be poetry evolved more from life and less from the Academy: accessible, intelligent poems with the virtues of Insider poetry, but something extra too. A group of poets whom I will call the Stand Up poets are writing that poetry now.

---

4 Donald Hall, "Poetry and Ambition," *AWP Newsletter* (February/March 1987): 1.
5 Ibid., 4.
6 Jack Miles, "Nobody Reads Poetry," *Los Angeles Times Book Review* (November 1, 1987, Book Reviews).

The term *Stand Up poet* was coined by California State University, Long Beach professors Gerald Locklin and Charles Stetler to describe Edward Field, whose first book, *Stand Up, Friend, With Me*,[7] was the Lamont Poetry Prize selection for 1962. Many of the poets I'll be discussing were influenced by Field, whom I consider the Father of Stand Up Poetry.

For better or worse, the term emphasizes a characteristic that sometimes leads this poetry to be dismissed: its sense of humor. "Stand Up" brings to mind "comic," a quality that is anathema to many Insiders. But the phrase "Stand Up" means more than comedy. Stand Up poets do use humor. They also write poems to be read aloud, and are often fine stand up performers of their work. Most important, though, the term implies honesty, courage, straightforwardness, as in "Stand up for your rights," "Stand up and be counted," "Stand up for what you believe," a "stand up guy." Stand Up poets write "stand up" poems: honest, brave, direct, unpretentious, strong.

Stand Up poets are found nationwide, but flourish in Southern California, an area famed for glitz and hype, and not smiled upon by Insiders. In this essay, I will use the work of Los Angeles area poets Ron Koertge, Elliot Fried, Gerald Locklin, Laurel Ann Bogen, and Suzanne Lummis, to represent Stand Up Poetry.

Because they cluster in LA, Stand Up poets are often lumped in with "street" poets of a strong anti-literary bent. This is a mistake. The five poets under discussion work with as much care as Insiders. Their educational background is also similar. Several are professors. Most have advanced degrees. Education and literacy are apparent in their work, even when it is most distinct from Insider poetry.

The five poets I will discuss have been highly successful in the world of the small press and "underground." They have, on occasion, been recognized by Insiders too. Ron Koertge has published a collection of poems with the University of Arkansas Press.[8] He was included in one national anthology, Edward Field's *A Geography of Poets*,[9] as were Gerald Locklin and Elliot Fried. Locklin is a cult figure in Germany. The work of all five poets, though, contains qualities that have kept them, finally, outside.

Each poet developed a strongly individual style independent of creative writing classes. None accepted the edicts of any school, or copied In

---

7 Edward Field, *Stand Up, Friend, With Me* (New York: Grove Press, 1963).

8 Ronald Koertge, *Life on the Edge of the Continent* (Fayetteville: University of Arkansas Press, 1982).

9 Edward Field, ed., *A Geography of Poets* (New York: Bantam Books, 1979).

teachers. They didn't know it at the time, but their choice meant that they would not have mentors to open doors for them, and that, however excellent their work might be, it would contain qualities that Insider editors and contest judges would detect and rule against.

I don't claim that any one characteristic is unique to Stand Up Poetry or absent from the work of all Insiders. Neither do I claim that every Stand Up poem contains every quality discussed below. I do claim, though, that the combination of qualities is unique, and characterizes Stand Up Poetry.

1. A sense of humor

All Stand Up poems are not funny; but they are often playful, irreverent, high-spirited, and fun, full of the techniques of comedy: good timing, absurd scenarios, hyperbole. This humor does not, however, equate to triviality. Nor does it imply, as "serious" Insiders sometimes assert, a "running from true emotion," "trivializing of experience," or pandering to "low" tastes.

In "Royce Newport Money," Ron Koertge writes of a gambler who had never won a bet in his life, and lost his clothes "betting / that a mummy would be next out of the restroom / at the House of Pies."[10] In "The Bells Are Ringing for Me and My Gal," Gerry Locklin writes of a Hare Krishna devotee who rings his doorbell, "I sympathize with bad skin, / having always had bad skin myself. / But that does not oblige me / to enjoy the sight of it at my front door."[11]

Laurel Ann Bogen's "Pygmy Headhunters and Killer Apes" finds the two groups playing basketball at the Y. "The Killer Apes win, but the Pygmy Headhunters are not sore / losers. They take the basketball home and boil it in your / cast iron pot."[12] Suzanne Lummis writes, in "To the Man in the Parking Lot at Sunset and Western," "I know my body's not enough. / I'll bring friends."[13]

Like many other modern artists, Stand Up poets choose humor as a device ideally suited to capture the absurdities, enormities, and pathos of modern life.

2. Performability

---

10 Koertge, *Life on the Edge of the Continent*, 8.

11 Gerald Locklin, *The Criminal Mentality* (Los Angeles: Red Hill Press, 1976): 33.

12 Laurel Ann Bogen, *Rag Tag We Kiss* (Los Angeles: Illuminati, 1989): 32.

13 Suzanne Lummis, "To the Man in the Parking Lot at Sunset and Western," in *In Danger* (Berkeley: Heyday Books, 1999): 20.

Many Stand Up poets have stage experience as actors or musicians, and most read their poems extremely well. Insider poets often pride themselves on a "flat" reading style, refusing to dramatize their work, and insisting that anything other than bare, uninflected words is dishonest. Stand Up poets don't agree. They write poems to read aloud, and read them with intensity and feeling. In person or in print, they aren't ashamed to entertain.

Laurel Ann Bogen reads her poems "The Night Grows Teeth"[14] with the fury of a Medea. Ron Koertge performs "The Seven Dwarfs, Each on His Deathbed, Remember Snow White,"[15] with the timing and poise of a headliner at the Comedy Store. Gerald Locklin performs his poem "Tap Dancing Lessons"[16] complete with demonstration, and sings "Cry" in a stentorian bass to conclude "I Never Liked Elvis Presley,"[17] a touching poem about childhood's end and the coming to grips with limitations.

Stand Up poets want poetry to be as enjoyable as a good movie or novel or piece of music, so they write poems that can be grasped, at least superficially, the first time through. This does not mean the poems are superficial. Good Stand Up Poetry stands up to close reading, too.

3. Clarity

Stand Up Poetry is clear and readable, easy and pleasurable to follow and comprehend. Stand Up poets don't use verbal smoke screens to disguise a lack of content, or avoid self-revelation. They do not confuse obscurity with depth. Historically, the best writers have always prized clarity; and with a few exceptions, the best literature has always been clear.

Doing psychotherapy with couples, I often use Ron Koertge's "What She Wanted," about a man who, to please his wife, gives her his bones until "Eventually I lay in a puddle / at her feet, only the boneless / penis waving like an anemone."[18] My clients—very few of whom were literature majors—never fail to understand and enjoy the poem. At the end, when the wife says, "Look at yourself. You're disgusting," they laugh (unless it hits too close to home), even as they see their relationship in a new light.

The profundity of a Stand Up poem is measured by the depth of its psychological and emotional truth, not by its difficulty of penetration.

---

14 Laurel Ann Bogen, *Do Iguanas Dance Under the Moonlight* (Los Angeles: Illuminati, 1984), 51.

15 Ronald Koertge, *Diary Cows* (Los Angeles: Little Caesar Press, 1981), 53.

16 Gerald Locklin, *Two for the Seesaw and One for the Road* (Stafford: Northwoods Press, 1980), 26.

17 Gerald Locklin, "I Never Liked Elvis Presley" (unpublished poem, 1989).

18 Koertge, *Life on the Edge of the Continent*, 49.

4. Flights of fancy

Stand Up poets are highly imaginative, able to "take off" from everyday events or observations to create strange, wondrous worlds. In "Poem Using the Words 'Wolves,' 'Corduroy,' and 'Bulgaria,'"[19] Suzanne Lummis springboards from those three words into a comically surreal and poignant story of marital misunderstanding and estrangement. In Bogen's "Mom and the Goldfish,"[20] an old woman in the projects finds a six-foot goldfish flopping down the street, and kidnaps him as a canasta partner. In Locklin's "The Leader of the Pack," the speaker leads a gang of bikers "except that we are all middle-aged, / have bad backs, / and ride Exercycles in formation."[21]

The unrestrained quality of the Stand Up poets' imaginative flights may jar the sensibilities of some Insiders, whose attitude can be like a crabby octogenarian demanding about an exuberant young person, "What's she on?" To less restricted personalities, however, the "trip" is mind-expanding in the best sense of the word.

5. Concern with human, not super-human, truth

Stand Up poets do not don the Seer's mantle before sitting down to write. They don't adopt the role of Poet as Prophet/Shaman. Stand Up poets are likely to see these poses as overcompensation for the public perception of Poet as Nonentity. Stand Up Poetry avoids the pompous and arcane for the earthy and accessible as when, in Koertge's "Ozymandias and Harriet,"[22] the Pharaoh keeps trying to assert that he is "King of Kings," while his wife interrupts and nags.

6. Natural language

Stand Up poets take seriously Wordsworth's statement that the language of poetry should be the language of people. They also agree with Yeats that if the poet's effort is visible, it's wasted. They craft their poems with such care that the poems may appear "tossed off," not crafted at all.

"The sharp carbolic smell of sweat adheres / to the low white room where my body works / the blue machines with names like Rotary Torso,

---

19 Suzanne Lummis, *Idiosyncrasies* (Los Angeles: Red Wind Books, 1989): 4.

20 Laurel Ann Bogen, *The Projects* (Los Angeles: Illuminati, 1987): 3.

21 Gerald Locklin, "The Leader of the Pack," *Wormwood Review 88* (1982): 142.

22 Ronald Koertge, *Men Under Fire* (Fallon: Duck Down Press, 1976): 32.

/ Duo Squat, and Double Chest," Elliot Fried writes in "Blue Machines."[23] In "Lilith," Ron Koertge writes: "God saw that he had made a mistake / and put [Adam] to sleep, wiped his brain / smooth as a grape, and tried again with / Eve, / who lay flat on her back, arms and / legs extended as if she had fallen from/ a tree . . ."[24]

Stand Up poets may purposely break lines on words like "the" and "and," or write prose poems to further break down poetic formality. Although their language can be rich, metaphoric, and musical, they avoid devices that heighten artificiality.

"I was laughing so hard I had to go outside and puke," Locklin declares in "Belly Laughs." "But don't you dare take that as a symbolic or psychoanalytic puke; / it was just the result of too many belly laughs, the sort one seldom / experiences after high school; by god, i went back in the bar / and laughed some more."[25]

7. A strong individual voice

Stand Up poets sound like actual people: interesting ones, with something to say. A random sampling of poems from "Younger American" anthologies[26] reveals numbing similarities in subject matter, sensibility, and style. Without names on the poems, it would be hard, in many cases, to say which poets wrote which poems.

Stand Up poets are not interchangeable, not afraid to have an individual voice. They don't choose neutral subjects and obscure language on the theory that what can't be pinned down can't be faulted. They are not interested in writing ego-less poems, or jewel-like word-clusters without heart or guts.

"The first symptom," Lummis warns in "Becoming an Ordinary Housewife," "is when you begin to beg forgiveness from household objects."[27] Stand Up poems speak with their readers, person to person.

8. A close relationship to fiction

---

23 Elliot Fried, "Blue Machines," *Poetry LA* 15 (1987): 1.

24 Koertge, *Diary Cows*, 60.

25 Locklin, *The Criminal Mentality*, 22.

26 *The Morrow Anthology of Younger American Poets* (Quill, 1985) will serve as an example.

27 Lummis, *Idiosyncrasies*, 8.

Stand Up poets are often accomplished writers of prose fiction, and make free use of the techniques of narrative prose. Koertge and Locklin have published novels. Bogen and Fried have published short fiction. Lummis has written several produced plays.

Not surprisingly, these poets favor story-poems. Locklin's "Goldie Girl"[28] is the story of a couple whose fights entertain a bored middle-class neighborhood. Bogen's "Gene Wilder Saved My Life"[29] tells how it happened.

While many poets concentrate on metrical tension, producing well-crafted, dramatically flaccid work, good Stand Up poets use conflict, hooks, reversals, character development, dialogue—the stuff of effective fiction—to create poems that grab readers and hold on.

"Sorrow," Adam says in Koertge's "Lilith," "I feel sorrow." "You eat too fast," says Eve. "It's gas."[30]

9. Wide open subject matter

Many poets—Insiders and Outsiders—draw their subjects from a limited pool. Poems about other poems abound, as well as poems about painting, music, sculpture—legitimate subjects, but smacking of artistic in-breeding. Titles are often solemn, staid, and dull.

As a teacher, I have found that a glance at the contents of prestigious contemporary anthologies produces groans from college students. On the other hand, Stand Up poets write about subjects of immediate interest. Even their titles are interesting: Bogen's "I Eat Lunch With a Schizophrenic,"[31] Locklin's "Toad Agonistes,"[32] Lummis's "The Woman in the Gold Cellophane Costume,"[33] Fried's "Message To Be Found in an Enormous Fortune Cookie,"[34] Koertge's "Things Which Make You so Scared You Can't Swallow and You Start to Cry and You Tell Them That You'll Do Anything if They'll Just Leave You Alone."[35]

At a poetry reading in LA, Tess Gallagher told how, driving down the Oregon coast, poet Mark Strand remarked that he was tired of student

28 Gerald Locklin, "Goldie Girl," *Wormwood Review*: 138.

29 Bogen, *The Projects*, 25.

30 Koertge, *Diary Cows*, 60.

31 Bogen, *Do Iguanas Dance Under the Moonlight*, 42.

32 Gerald Locklin, *Poop and Other Poems* (Long Beach: Mag Press, 1972): 57.

33 Lummis, *Idiosyncrasies*, 20.

34 Elliot Fried, *Picking Up the Pieces* (Salem: Rumba Train Press, 1975): 33.

35 Ronald Koertge, *Twelve Photographs of Yellowstone* (Los Angeles: Red Hill Press, 1976): 13.

poems about grandfathers and relatives. "Why doesn't someone write a poem about linoleum?" he asked.

What he wanted sounds like a Stand Up poem. Subjects like Fried's "The Sensuous Dog,"[36] Bogen's "Mosquito Control,"[37] Lummis's "Cockroaches,"[38] Locklin's "An Excedrin Hard-On,"[39] may at first glance seem silly, dirty, not serious, unpoetic as linoleum. But Stand Up poets take seriously the fact that the majority of people's lives are spent far removed from the sublime. They embrace the ridiculous, the banal, the mundane, and find poems waiting there.

10. Use of urban and pop culture

Historically, poets have been preoccupied with Nature. Most Stand Up poets, though, were born and raised in cities. The imagery most natural to them is not meadows and woods, lakes and starry skies, but parking lots and smog, supermarkets, freeways, malls, and fast-food stands. Just as nature poets use streams and fields, Stand Up poets use the city as a backdrop against which larger human issues stand revealed. Stand Up poems may satirize the modern world and popular culture, but they revel in it, too: the brand names, the day-to-day activities with cleansers and deodorants. In "Smells,"[40] Ron Koertge creates a toilet bowl deodorant called "Flush Me Not." In "To Condo,"[41] Fried conjugates a new verb of the modern age. In "The Great Orange Leonard Scandal,"[42] Bogen chronicles the rise and fall of a franchise giant. Writers of Stand Up poems use our culture's icons, as poets have always done, to dramatize and illuminate.

11. Recharging cliché

The modern world is built upon cliché. How could it be otherwise, when mass media ensure that today's fresh line ("Make my day"; "May the force be with you") is on everyone's lips by tomorrow. Ezra Pound's directive "Make it new" has been twisted into a Creative Writing fetish, where "newness" is praised at the expense of clarity, aptness, sense, and where any-

---

36 Elliot Fried, *This Poem Is Rated X* (Long Beach: Ersatz Press, 1972): 24.

37 Bogen, *The Projects*, 27.

38 Suzanne Lummis, "Cockroaches" (unpublished poem, 1989).

39 Locklin, *Poop and Other Poems*, 4.

40 Ronald Koertge, *The Father Poems* (Fremont: The Sumac Press, 1973): 37.

41 Elliot Fried, *The Man Who Owned Cars* (Long Beach: Deep River Press, 1984): 16.

42 Bogen, *The Projects*, 15.

thing that has ever been said before is damned as "unimaginative" and "cliché"—two words as feared as cancer.

Stand Up poets "make it new" by embracing cliché, finding new meaning and vitality in the stale phrases and perceptions that loom so large in our conversation and our lives. In Koertge's "These Students Couldn't Write . . ."[43] we see students literally unable to write their way out of a wet paper bag. In "Confessional Poem,"[44] Lummis involves her protagonist, "a file clerk and famous beauty," with a living cliché—a wealthy Doctor who peers into the valves of a plastic model heart "searching for love."

12. Celebration of the visceral
Stand Up poets write about death and sex and love and body functions. Their poems are strongly and overtly sexual. They glory in the fact that nice people eat and shit and sweat and fuck and bleed.

"Hemorrhoids are cranky as babies," Koertge writes in "Three Remedies." "The inside of the body / has ventured out, and no one there to greet it! Naturally it / is miffed . . ."[45] In poems such as Locklin's "Beer,"[46] Bogen's "Love of Shoe,"[47] Fried's "Striptease,"[48] they celebrate the body with directness and unabashed eroticism.

13. A youthful quality
Stand Up poets shun the stodgy for the fresh, the joyous, the fun, in poems such as Locklin's "Poop," where the poet's small daughter recites "Our pooper who art in poopland, hallowed be thy poop."[49]

Not surprisingly, such poems are dismissed as "juvenile" or "immature" by critics who adopt the voice of Parental Doom. Yet Poetry, as Thoreau said, should strike off chains, not clamp down more. Good Stand Up Poetry is a breath of liberation.

14. In your face, "good taste"
Stand Up poems dare to be rambunctious, excitable, immoderate, exuberant, at a time when most writers and editors seem terrified of appearing

---

43 Koertge, *Life on the Edge of the Continent*, 60.

44 Lummis, *Idiosyncrasies*, 11.

45 Koertge, *Diary Cows*, 43.

46 Locklin, *Poop and Other Poems*, 17.

47 Bogen, *The Projects*, 11.

48 Elliot Fried, *Striptease* (Long Beach: Applezaba Press, 1979): 4.

49 Locklin, *Poop and Other Poems*, 12.

unseemly, and consequently, the fashionable poetic stance is understated, proper, distant, detached. Stand Up poets risk telling unpopular truths about the world, and unflattering truths about themselves. By their choice of subjects, they risk appearing silly, crass, sentimental, perverse. In Lummis's "Breasts," a woman admits "I'm obsessed with Mark Eden Bust Developer advertisements."[50] In Bogen's "27 Years of Madness,"[51] a woman tells what it was like. In Locklin's "On the Rack," a man admits how he plays on a woman's insecurities to "keep her anxious, humble, and dependent."[52] In Fried's "Daily I Fall in Love with Waitresses,"[53] a man confesses his secret longing.

Stand Up poets risk irking, upsetting, frightening, offending. But their risks pay off in daring and enjoyable poetry.

15. American values

Without being jingoistic, Stand Up poets are American in the best sense of the word. They love to deflate sacred cows—including Poetry and themselves. They celebrate the human. They love laughter and hate hypocrisy, identifying with and rooting for the underdog. In poems such as Locklin's "basketball,"[54] Bogen's "Rat City,"[55] Koertge's "Roy and Dale,"[56] Fried's "Ascension at Hof's,"[57] these poets celebrate American food, American entertainment, American habits, American landscapes, American dreams.

General Comments

As educated people, the Stand Up poets have been influenced by the classics, from Aristophanes to Shakespeare, Ovid to Milton, Blake, Wordsworth, Hardy, Donne. More recent influences include Walt Whitman, T. S. Eliot, Ezra Pound, W. C. Williams, the Beats, Dylan Thomas, Sylvia Plath, and Elizabeth Bishop. Among contemporaries, Stand Up poets' individual tastes vary widely, from Edward Field and Charles Bukowski, to Mark Strand, Galway Kinnell, Donald Justice, James Tate, Russell Edson, Sharon Olds, Stephen Dunn, David Bottoms, Philip Dacey, and many more.

---

50 Lummis, *Idiosyncrasies*, 23.

51 Bogen, *Do Iguanas Dance Under the Moonlight*, 21.

52 Gerald Locklin, *On the Rack* (Parkdale: Trout Creek Press, 1988): 3.

53 Elliot Fried, *The Man Who Owned Cars* (Long Beach: Deep River Press, 1984): 14.

54 Locklin, *Poop and Other Poems*, 25.

55 Bogen, *Do Iguanas Dance Under the Moonlight*, 44.

56 Koertge, *Diary Cows*, 62.

57 Fried, *The Man Who Owned Cars*, 33.

Although I have presented the Stand Up poets as a group, they are not an organized "school." Their writing ranges from expansive to spare, from rhapsodic to dry, from surreal to very real. They are individuals, drawn together by certain shared sensibilities, but not a common style.

Ron Koertge uses outrageous and comic metaphors, as well as lyrical ones to create poems that move between hilarity and surprising sweetness. His use of pop culture is masterful, while his Midwest background is apparent in his choice of imagery.

Gerald Locklin is the least traditionally poetic of the lot. His work sparks the debate "Is this poetry?" His voice is frank, direct, and wryly intellectual. He uses twenty-letter and four-letter words in the same breath, and focuses on narrative, not metaphor. His poems are visceral, and often aphoristic.

Laurel Ann Bogen is the most overtly passionate of the group. Her poems are full of madness and love. She writes most obviously out of the oral tradition, with a great deal of emphasis on sound, and is a riveting performer.

Suzanne Lummis is slyly feminine. Her poems are quirky, witty, subtly sexual. An actress and playwright, her poems often read like dramatic monologues. She uses Los Angeles in the way that nature poets use nature, as a backdrop against which larger human issues stand revealed.

Eliot Fried has a biting wit, and is a keen observer of the American scene, especially as embodied in Southern California. His poems range from the scathing and satiric to the quietly poignant.

These poets' talent has not gone unacknowledged. Besides publishing widely with small presses, they have published in journals including *American Scholar*, *Western Humanities Review*, *The Literary Review*, and *Poetry Now*. Several have been finalists in national Insider competitions. Response to their work at readings is enthusiastic and exuberant.

Critical response is a different matter. There has been little of it. Locklin and Koertge have each won the *Wormwood Review* Award for the most unrecognized poetry book of merit published in a given year—a plaudit that underscores the lack of national attention. "There's a casualness to your language that I enjoy as a reader, although it's this same quality that makes me reluctant to publish your work," an editor wrote to Koertge. Presumably, if the poems had been more formal and less enjoyable, the editor would have rushed to publish them. But, judging from the sales figures of that editor's and similar magazines, readers would not have rushed to read them.

Conclusion

History has shown that the art most praised by the contemporary Establishment is likely to be quickly forgotten. If this holds true, Outsiders are writing the poems that history will judge our era's best. I'm writing this to call attention to a kind of poetry that I believe history will judge more favorably.

If American poetry is to achieve a readership beyond the confines of creative writing class, poets must write poems that appeal to lovers of the other arts: intelligent laypersons living in the non-Creative-Writing world.

Stand Up poets are writing those poems now.

In Defense of Clarity

A strange thing happened to me this week. I sat through two forty-five-min-ute poetry readings on two consecutive days, and my mind didn't wander once. The poets were Billy Collins and Ron Koertge; and alright, maybe my mind did wander once. I remember wondering how long Koertge had been going, and hoping he'd go on some more.

I didn't search the room for friends. I didn't check my watch. I didn't think about my income tax, or the leak in my left front tire, or what I'd have for dinner that night. I climbed on board the poems and rode, de-lighted to be there.

I attend at least twenty-five poetry readings a year. I read a minimum of twenty poems a week (not counting students' work) in books and mag-azines. And while I'm doing it, my mind fidgets like an ADHD child. Getting through a whole poem often takes an act of will. Most readings feel like time in jail. I persevere because to find a poem I like—much less a poet—makes the fidgeting worthwhile.

But it shouldn't be so hard. I love to read. I have two degrees in English, an MFA in creative writing, and a PhD in counseling psychology. I've taught English and creative writing at the university level for a dozen years, edited a literary magazine, co-edited an anthology. In my work as a psycho-therapist, I follow rambling client narratives, teasing out hidden themes and meanings. If my mind wanders during a poem—often refusing to come back—it's not because I'm insufficiently motivated, or too dunder-headed to cope with poetry. Something is wrong with the poetry that I find. And that something was very right in Collins's and Koertge's poems.

It's no secret that poetry is in trouble in the United States. The only people who deny this are poets. Yet, except for them, and a dwindling number of non-poet professors, almost no one reads the stuff anymore. As far back as the 1950s, poet Karl Shapiro wrote of "the sickness of modern poetry." Across the Atlantic, Philip Larkin saw the same sickness, and named the same pathogen: the literary critic/professor/poet.

Though I'm all three of those things, I agree. I believe that large contingents of the "academy" have gone seriously astray, championing poems as stunted and dysfunctional as a bound foot.

So why do Collins's and Koertge's poems sprint to my brain's Pleasure Center, while most contemporary poems hobble or fall flat? Their wit, keen perceptions, and fine sense of metaphor certainly help. But the catalyst that makes everything work is clarity.

By this I don't mean simply "ease of understanding." There are, it seems to me, four interrelated levels of literary clarity.

1. Surface clarity
2. Imagistic clarity
3. Dramatic clarity
4. Psychological clarity

In a poem with *surface clarity*, the reader always knows what's going on. Wordiness, stilted phrasings, and anything else that clouds the verbal air, are shunned. The language of the poem doesn't need translating or deciphering.

In a poem with *imagistic clarity*, imagery is sharp and memorable, like Van Gogh's crows, Michelangelo's David, Keats's Grecian urn. Figurative language is striking, apt, and illuminating, not strained, inaccurate, or perfunctory. Poems with imagistic clarity change how we perceive the world. Poems without it seem unfocused, vague, inconsequential. Readers finish such poems struggling to remember what they've read.

Poems with *dramatic clarity* have a clear sense of momentum and purpose. They often root the reader in a specific place, and when they do, let him know why he is there. Such poems work like good stories, pulling the reader along surely and confidently to the end. They don't bog down with unnecessary details. They don't wander aimlessly. They are not desultory or afraid of strong emotion. Each line makes us eager to read the next.

Psychological clarity is the deepest clarity, underlying and supporting the other three. To a psychotherapist, this clarity is the *sine qua non* of mental health. People who don't see and feel clearly are neurotic[58] by defi-

---

58 A "neurotic" disorder is one in which " ... the patient distorts (but does not deny) reality." Raymond Corsini, *Current Psychotherapies* (Itasca: F.E. Peacock Publishers, 1984): 553.

nition, their lives subject to missteps caused by their distortions of the world. Poets who don't see and feel clearly are doomed to many missteps in their poems.

As I reflected on Collins's and Koertge's work, a theorem came to mind: *The best poets see the world most clearly, and express most clearly what they see.* This theorem led me to a corollary: *Mediocre poets see the world un-clearly and/or don't express clearly what they see.* Their poetry, like neurotic perception, is unclear. Such poets write as if they needed psychotherapy.[59]

Needing therapy is no black mark against a writer. Kafka certainly had his "issues;" Sylvia Plath was the quintessential "crazy poet." Yet their best work, even when it is strange, is very clear.

For years, however, there has been a tendency among contemporary poets and critics to disdain clarity. Rather than state directly "I'm against clarity," or "I support obscurity,"[60] the anti-clarity forces speak of poems as "richly textured," "complex," "challenging," "dense," "allusive," "elliptical," or simply "difficult." They may even claim that opaque works are clear, implying "if you're smart enough to see." Declaring poetry an art reserved, necessarily, for the few,[61] they justify the dull, the muddled, the baffling, and dismiss or castigate the occasional heretic who faults contemporary poets, not inept readers, for the plight of contemporary poetry.

The Modernist shake-up of poetry is well-understood. Striving to render new, complex realities, Pound, Eliot, Stevens, et al. created difficult masterpieces—and sparked an onslaught of obscurity. Since fewer people could now tell wheat from chaff, those who claimed the ability donned the mantle of Authority. This created another strong push away from clarity. Just as priests enshrined themselves as necessary Interpreters of Holy Writ, professor-critics enshrined themselves as necessary Interpreters of Texts.[62]

---

59 "Poetry is an affair of sanity, of seeing things as they are [i.e., clearly]. The less a writer's work approximates to this maxim, the less claim he has on the attention of his contemporaries and of posterity." Philip Larkin, *Required Writing* (New York: Farrar, Straus, Giroux, 1983): 197.

60 The so-called "L=A=N=G=U=A=G=E" poets and some surrealists may be exceptions to this rule.

61 ". . . most people of today, of whatever social level, no matter what kind of education they have access to . . . are incapable of responding to poetry." Jascha Kessler, "The Challenge of Poetry," *Poets & Writers* (January/February 1990): 35.

62 "The modern critic has pulled criticism up by the bootstraps to a position of cultural power which in the twentieth century is staggering. No wonder all those bright young men want to be critics . . ." Karl Shapiro, *In Defense of Ignorance* (New York: Random House, 1960), 8.

Older poems had needed interpretation, not because the writing wasn't clear, but because it incorporated archaic language, references, and beliefs that readers no longer understood.[63] Now, modern professor-critics took "difficult" modern texts and, by interpreting them in difficult ways, left almost everyone behind. "We can say that modern criticism thrives on the difficult—either on explaining the difficult or explaining that what seemed straightforward is in fact difficult,"[64] wrote Philip Larkin. The result is that, today, even highly educated people view poetry as an oppressive Mystery that must be interpreted to be understood, and that is guaranteed to make them feel inadequate and bored.[65]

No wonder readers stay away.

As the 1900s passed the halfway mark, another literary force was growing: the professor-poet. Raised on the values of modern criticism and, increasingly, French literary theory, these hyphenates continued the trend away from clear poetry.[66]

The rise of creative writing programs has had a major impact on poetry. But the current plague of mediocre poets is not the fault of the workshop. Little League has loosed millions of would-be ballplayers on the world, without diluting the quality of the Major Leagues.

For a time, creative writing workshops actually reversed the trend toward obscurity, moving some poetry back toward at least surface clarity. But deeper levels of clarity were still ignored. Cut off from the non-aca-

---

63 "We seem to have forgotten that the reader in Dante's age knew what Dante was referring to . . . Homer's audience didn't have to consult Bullfinch's Age of Fable to find out what Homer meant. We in the twentieth century seem to think that those Greek and Italian audiences must have been almost as learned as Sir James Frazer; we seem to accept the fact that we cannot understand the poet unless someone tells us what he means." Ibid., 20.

64 Larkin, *Required Writing*, 168.

65 [As for] "Textbooks designed for the "understanding" or "exploration" of poetry . . . My experience with students who have been subjected to these dry and terrible tomes, the very paper of which seems impregnated with lead, is that they are utterly and permanently stunned into literary insensibility." Shapiro, *In Defense of Ignorance*, 12.

66 ". . . it is hardly an exaggeration to say that the poet has gained the happy position wherein he can praise his own poetry in the press and explain it in the class-room, and the reader has been bullied into giving up the consumer's power to say 'I don't like this, bring me something different.' Let him now so much as breathe a word about not liking a poem, and he is in the dock before he can say Edwin Arlington Robinson. And the charge is a grave one: flabby sensibility, insufficient or inadequate critical tools, and inability to meet new verbal and emotional situations. Verdict: guilty, plus a few riders on the prisoner's mental upbringing, addiction to mass amusements, and enfeebled responses. It is time some of you playboys realized, says the judge, that reading a poem is hard work. Fourteen days in stir. Next case." Larkin, *Required Writing*, 81.

demic world, workshop poetry began to evolve in odd and, to Outsiders, unappealing ways.

Adherents of the "I don't know what it means, but I love how it sounds" approach, for instance, assume that the poet is primarily a musician, and that to be much concerned with meaning is to be a philistine. This belief leads straight to obscurity.

Of course sound is important in poetry. The "music" of vowels and consonants is enjoyable, and makes for memorable phrases. The rhythm of words goes deeper still, touching primal forces in us all. Moreover, the unconscious mind often uses sound-associations to lead us toward poetic discoveries, and should be encouraged to do so. However, judging from many poems I see, following sound has led the poet to a muddle, and an abdication of clarity.

Sound is not the primary power of words. Listen to a language very different from your own, and you may even find the sounds annoying. Listen to the perorations of politicians and preachers, and see what rhythm amounts to, stripped of meaning. Music deals with sound for its own sake. Poetry uses sound to help reach meaning—not a Cliff Notes paraphrase, but the totality of what the poem communicates. To make sound the most important part of poetry is like saying, "The best part of sex is the bed."

Another common, albeit unvoiced, workshop "value" requires emotion to be distanced by a process similar to neurotic dissociation. Middle class Americans, the population from which most of our poets and critics are drawn, have never been comfortable with strong displays of emotion. In poetry, as in their lives, they do their best to keep such feelings at bay—thereby producing neurotic symptoms in their lives and their verse.

Showing strong emotion, or even taking a heartfelt position, opens the heart to criticism and attack. Like children in troubled families, poets learn to disguise and dissimulate, keeping the upsetting or controversial at a safe distance. In this way, they limit criticism of their poetry to matters of technique—far less threatening than discussions of the poet's heart. The result is uncommitted, safely obscure poetry.

Workshops almost universally advocate "fresh imagery" and "specific details." This is good advice in theory, and should add to clarity. In practice, "fresh" imagery too often means strained and obtuse figurative language and bizarre juxtapositions that play havoc with clarity. Specific details are often used haphazardly, in hopes, one assumes, that the Unconscious will create meaning from chaos.

This rarely happens if the poet lacks psychological clarity. Instead, the imagery obscures the picture, and the details cancel each other out, diminishing imagistic clarity, demolishing dramatic clarity, and never approaching psychological clarity.

Yet contemporary apologists still parrot the Modernist maxim that complex (i.e., obscure) poetry is necessary to express the complex emotional and psychological states characteristic of the complex modern world. How can poetry be clear, they ask, when the modern world is not?

This is the Fallacy of Imitative Form. Writing neurotically does not illuminate neurosis. Losing the reader in textual confusion does not illuminate a confusing world.

Joseph Duemer[67] speaks of "admirable obscurity," and "necessary obscurity," claiming that it may lead to emotional clarity. I think he means— to use my terminology—that a poem with a cloudy surface may still possess imagistic, dramatic, and psychological clarity. In theory, I agree. Eliot's *The Waste Land* is such a poem. But in most cases, obscurity is neither necessary nor admirable; it is the mark of insufficient psychological development, and/or fear of self-revelation, and/or fuzzy thinking, and/or adherence to fashion, and/or lack of talent, and/or a weak effort willing to stop short of poetic truth.

The greatest insights, scientific and philosophical, are clear. "Do unto others as you would have them do unto you." "All suffering comes from attachment." $E=mc^2$. Newton's Laws. Galileo's model of the universe. Even the Heisenberg Uncertainty Principle, often cited by indeterminists, is a clear principle. The mark of genius is the ability to tease out these clear and relatively simple principles from the vast confusion of data that bombards us as we pick our way through the world. That is the scientist's and the artist's job. For poets to do their part, they must be clear.

Duemer writes of poetic "reticence"[68] as if it were a stylistic master stroke. But would a musician be applauded if he played everything pianissimo because he was too shy to bang the keys? People seek psychotherapy when they're too shy, too anxious, too blocked, too "reticent" to see their own truth, much less articulate it clearly. I applaud the courage of their struggle, just as I applaud the courage of a would-be pilot struggling with a fear of heights. But airline passengers, and readers, deserve more.

---

67 Joseph Duemer, "The Poetics of Awkwardness," *THE Journal* 13, no. 2 (1990): 82–95.
68 Duemer, "The Poetics of Awkwardness," 87.

Another common defense of poetic obscurity is the claim that clarity rules out "mystery." But life itself is a mystery. That E does equal mc^2 is a mystery. I could cite numerous examples, but will allow Ezra Pound's "The Return"[69] (readily available on the Internet) to suffice: haunting, mysterious, and clear.

Neither does clarity rule out complexity, or that quality much-beloved of literary critics: ambiguity.[70] Eliot's "The Love Song of J. Alfred Prufrock" is complex, especially to a reader not familiar with modern poetry. Prufrock himself is full of ambiguities. But the images in the poem are clear; the drama is clear. And Prufrock's character is heartbreakingly clear—one of the best portraits ever made of a reticent, ambivalent man.

Perhaps the most frequent, pernicious, and false accusation against clarity equates it *a priori* with a lack of depth. To quote Duemer again, "Many of [C. K.] Williams's earlier poems . . . might have landed comfortably in Steve Kowit's *The Maverick Poets* [an anthology of accessible poems] where they would have been among the very best in the anthology, possessing as they do *a philosophical depth completely lacking in most of the mavericks* [italics mine]."[71]

The obscure poem, on the other hand, is assumed to be profound.

The clear poem at least puts the goods on the table. The obscure poem hides what likely isn't there.

Two short poems, "Embrace" by Billy Collins, and "What She Wanted" by Ron Koertge, demonstrate the philosophical, psychological, and emotional depth that can be found in clear poetry.

First, Collins's poem:

Embrace

You know the parlor trick.
Wrap your arms around your own body
and from the back it looks like
someone is embracing you,
her hands grasping your shirt,
her fingernails teasing your neck.

69 Ezra Pound, *Selected Poems* (New York: New Directions, 1957): 24.
70 "Ambiguity is one of the favorite principles of the modern critic, but this one has backfired rather badly, killing quite a few graduate students." Shapiro, *In Defense of Ignorance*,16.
71 Duemer, "The Poetics of Awkwardness," 94.

From the front it is another story.
You never looked so alone,
your crossed elbows and screwy grin.
You could be waiting for a tailor
to fit you with a straitjacket,
one that would hold you really tight.[72]

"Embrace" demonstrates all four levels of clarity. The language is easy to follow (surface clarity). The imagery is sharp and memorable (imagistic clarity), and the poem moves with a strong sense of purpose from beginning to end (dramatic clarity). It's in the area of psychological clarity, though, that the poem shines most brightly.

Collins addresses the human need for love, and the need to provide for oneself that comfort which the world does not. On the one hand, this is healthy and life-affirming; on the other, it is unhealthy and sad. The truth is that we're all in the world alone, and must love ourselves before anyone else can. The truth is also that we don't want to; we want others' love to make us feel worthy and fulfilled. Collins's poem expresses that duality.

The poem deals, too, with illusion and perspective. From one angle, the scene described looks passionate; from another, it looks "goofy." That's the way love is for lovers and observers alike. One moment it looks wonderful; the next, ludicrous. The straitjacket image adds another contrast. Love constricts us at the same time it makes us feel secure. Love is crazy in some senses; and it keeps us from running amok.

Collins's simple language is, at the same time, rich and evocative. Comparing love to a "parlor trick" points to the ways in which we deceive ourselves by "falling" into it. Furthermore, to do a parlor trick, there has to be a parlor. We require leisure and the wealth to spend time fretting about love. Our Western obsession is not universal—or, necessarily, good.

The words "grasping" and "teasing" convey pleasure and pain just as love does. "Crossed elbows" signify a "closed posture"—closed to relationships, and also self-protective. Ranging farther afield, one may think of "crossbones," an image both of death and romantic piracy.

The "screwy grin" conveys sexual overtones. And the idea that "a tailor" must be hired to imprison us speaks volumes about modern love (where marriage can be a costly prison), and the modern world, where we must

---

72 Billy Collins, *The Apple That Astonished Paris* (Fayetteville: The University of Arkansas Press, 1988): 52.

constantly pay for things that make us miserable. Being held "really tight" can be good or bad, depending on who is holding, and when. Even the word "tight," implying "securely" and "passionately" and "restrictively" and "drunk," has contradictory—and mutually reinforcing—connotations.

Collins's "clear" poem, then, is loaded with ambiguity: the enlightening, not the baffling kind. When I've read the poem to audiences, they invariably laugh at the last line—a laugh not of hilarity, but of painful recognition. Few would be able, on the spot, to articulate all of the poem's multiple meanings. They don't need to. Their laughter indicates an intuitive grasp of the poem's striking central metaphor—a sense that it accurately depicts "the way it is." That constitutes psychological clarity.

Now, Koertge's poem:

> What She Wanted
>
> was my bones. As I gave them
> to her one at a time she put
> them in a bag from Saks.
> As long as I didn't hesitate
> she collected scapula and
> vertebrae with a smile.
>
> If I grew reluctant she pouted.
> Then I would come across with
> rib cage or pelvis.
>
> Eventually I lay in a puddle
> at her feet, only the boneless
> penis waving like an anemone.
> "Look at yourself," she said.
> "You're disgusting."[73]

"What She Wanted" looks even simpler than Collins's poem. Again the language is easy to follow; the imagery is sharp and memorable; the poem moves with a strong sense of purpose. Again, the poem is psychologically complex, and absolutely clear.

---

73 Koertge, *Life on the Edge of the Continent*, 49.

Freud voiced the question men have asked since the first woman criticized the cave her mate had fought a 1000-pound bear to get for her: "What do women want?" Koertge answers that they want men's bones.

"Bones" implies the essence of a man: what keeps him strong (*backbone*) and potent (*boner*). In the relationship described, the woman wants a strong, potent man to love. But she also wants his strength for herself—both because she thinks she lacks it, and because he can use it to oppose her.

The man, out of a neurotic need to please her and keep her love, tries to give her what she wants. Little by little, he overtaxes and diminishes himself, putting his offerings in a bag "from Saks." Since neurotic people may judge their worth by the value of gifts they're given, and judge a gift's value by where it was bought, a gift from Saks tells the woman 1. that the man is successful, and 2. that she is valuable—more valuable than if the man merely gives of himself.

Periodically, the woman checks her mate for feedback. If he seems willing to give more, she increases her demands; if he seems "reluctant," she "pouts"—withdrawing the love and approval that the man craves. Eventually, he "comes across" with more "bones" until, having lost everything that made her love him, he lies in "a puddle" at her feet. (We speak of "melting" into a "puddle of love." We also speak of the puppy making "a puddle.")

Even the penis has lost its potency, as often happens when a man has lost his self-esteem. But the penis is not completely flaccid. It still waves like a grotesque, pathetic flower, not erect enough to be effective, just enough to call attention to itself.

The clinical accuracy of this picture is startling. By the end of the poem, both man and woman see the man as disgusting. The woman has won—i.e., gotten what she wanted; and she has lost, having helped to destroy the man she loved.

I used to teach an adult-school class called "Understanding Men." To start the class, I would chalk "What She Wanted" on the blackboard. Every time, as I wrote out the last lines, I would hear a kind of collective gasp from the class as the force of Koertge's metaphor hit home. That is the power of psychological clarity.

It would seem logical now to take an obscure poem and prove that it lacks clarity and therefore fails as a poem. The trouble is, no one bad poem can stand for all the rest. And failure, like Duemer's "philosophical depth," is always a judgment call. What I suggest is that each reader examine a prestigious contemporary anthology or literary journal. If you decide that the poetry deserves its prestige, I have no wish to convince you otherwise. But if you agree with me that much prestige poetry is unclear and unrewarding, the question arises: Why don't more people scream, "The emperor has no clothes!"?

In fact, they do. Readers scream it nationwide by walking, poem-less, from bookstores. This would tell publishers something was wrong, if publishers expected poetry to sell. They don't.[74] When poetry books lose money, publishers simply shake their collective heads, as if to say, "What did we expect?"

Still, a few people read contemporary poems. Why don't *they* announce that the emperor has no clothes?

Many don't because, like the emperor's subjects in the famous story, they're ashamed. Everyone knows that it takes intelligence and sensitivity to understand a poem. Who wants to look dull and insensitive? Better to smile and applaud as the poem struts by. Better to convince yourself there is something to see.

Besides these defensive appreciators, there is a more aggressive group. Often poets themselves, they adopt a more-discerning-than-thou posture, like musicologists who turn their noses up at Beethoven's *Fifth* in favor of his Sonata for Triangle and Pig's Bladder. This posture is common among critics. Some take the stance that only the writer and they are clever enough to grasp a difficult poem; others, that they're *more* clever than the poet—and, in the case of deconstructionists, more creative too.

It doesn't take a Freud to see that the issue isn't art; it's self-esteem. Even the most successful poets don't make as much money as a moderately successful doctor, lawyer, or CPA. But poets may be just as bright, and even more ambitious. They try to balance lower pay and the public's apathy with strong doses of ego-gratification. They tell themselves and each other that they are more intelligent, more sensitive, more discerning, more spontaneous, more artistic, more in touch with the unconscious, more politically correct and sincere and morally upright, and all-in-all, just better people than almost anyone. They proclaim themselves Emperors of Poetry, and never acknowledge—or apparently, perceive—their nakedness.

---

74 ". . . the assumption now is that no one will read it [poetry], and wouldn't understand or enjoy it if they did." Larkin, *Required Writing*, 80.

The few people who scream, "I see the Emperor's bare butt!" are—or quickly find themselves—on the fringe of the poetry scene, their screams consigned to "little" mags of small circulation, which Emperors ignore.

Why should Emperors want to change the status quo?[75] They teach two or three small classes a year, and make a good salary doing it. Their work appears in the "best" places. They can travel, giving readings, if they like. They wield the power to confer favors, and make or break careers. Within their small circle, they are admired, catered to. And they get to be in a very exclusive club.

The AMA and the Bar work to advance and protect members. The Emperors' Club does too. Members praise each other in print, hire each other for important readings and professorships, publish each other, award each other fellowships and prizes, and react with high moral and intellectual outrage to any challenge. American Scholar editor Joseph Epstein was excoriated in the *AWP Chronicle* for his essay "Who Killed Poetry?"[76] I don't agree with everything Epstein said, but I was struck by the fury with which well-known poets attacked him for daring to state publicly that something is rotten in the state of poetry. If Epstein had been a poet, he would have been a target for career-sabotage.[77]

Like self-esteem, "career" is a key to understanding U.S. poetry today. Poetry books don't make money, but publishing in the "right" places translates into grants and teaching jobs, which do. Some successful up-and-comers decide, in cold blood, where they need to publish, then do whatever it takes: copying the prevailing style and subject matter, playing court to editors, trading favors, schmoozing like Hollywood agents, none of which improves their poetry.

It's doubtful if the talents required to get into the Emperors' Club correlate with a talent for poetry. The quickest way into The Club is to

---

75 "What can be done about this? Who wants anything done about it? Certainly not the poet, who is in the unprecedented position of peddling both his work and the standard by which it is judged. Certainly not the new reader, who, like a partner of some unconsummated marriage, has no idea of anything better." Larkin, *Required Writing*, 82.

76 Joseph Epstein, "Who Killed Poetry?" *The Writer's Chronicle*, (1989): 1–17.

77 Carolyn Kizer writes how poet Karl Shapiro's assertions that American poetry was "sick," "maimed," "crumbling under the pressures of criticism," "murdered," indeed "dead" damaged his standing and career over the years. "Did Shapiro then expect his colleagues to rush up and thank him for saying that their life's work was a bootless enterprise and their own work worthless, and smother him with kisses? One can't help believing that these repeated asseverations are part of his own literary death wish." Carolyn Kizer, review of *Reports of My Death* by Karl Shapiro, *Los Angeles Times*, May 13, 1990.

land—usually via a creative writing program—a mentor who is already there. And how does one do that? Not usually by writing better than the mentor. Not usually by having the unique vision that comes with psychological clarity, and without which one can't write good poetry.

Students excel in most creative writing classes the same way they do in other classes: by pleasing the teacher. The fastest rising stars in contemporary poetry are the good girls and boys of the big-name creative writing programs. Sincere, concerned, ambitious, they steer judiciously toward the middle ground (or whatever terrain their teacher favors), avoiding controversy, writing the kind of poetry Steve Kowit calls "tepid, mannered, and opaque."[78] Long after they have graduated and moved into successful poetry careers, they hand poems in to the "right" magazines as dutifully as they handed in term papers in school. In print, they describe each other's poems as "urgent," "essential," "necessary." Only a churl would answer, "Not to me."

The poets I reference seem to be, in the main, decent people. Some have talent. But like lawyers, doctors, and MBAs fresh out of school, most seem cast in the same Jell-O mold. Even well into middle-age, their poetic vision conforms to the company line. They write as their mentors did, and wear no clothes.

Sounds grim, I know. But there is hope. Sometime in almost everyone's life, he or she is moved—by love, sadness, loneliness, some strong emotion—to pick up a book of poetry. Usually the book is put down quickly, with another reader lost. But the impulse was there. All that's needed to hook readers are poems that they won't want to put down: poems capable of adding clarity and pleasure to their lives.

That kind of poetry would help English departments too, bringing more students to study—not just write—poetry.

What is required is revolution;[79] and those are bloody, and take time. The Emperors of Poetry are well-entrenched, ready for battle. Most of the "best" journals and publishers are on their side. But the revolt is underway. Revolutionary poems are being written all the time—not inspired by the

---

78 Steve Kowit, *The Maverick Poets* (Santee: Gorilla Press, 1988).

79 "If the medium [of poetry] is in fact to be rescued from among our duties and restored to our pleasures, I can only think that a large-scale revulsion has got to set in against present notions, and that it will have to start with poetry readers asking themselves more frequently whether they do in fact enjoy what they read, and, if not, what the point is of carrying on." Larkin, *Required Writing*, 82.

wish to conquer, but by the wish to touch readers, and in the best musical sense of the word, to play.

Some of these poems are being written by poets in The Club; some, by poets partway in; some by Outsiders. Steve Kowit's anthology *The Maverick Poets*[80] features a lot of this clear, revolutionary poetry. So does *Stand Up Poetry: An Expanded Anthology*.[81]

When I present this poetry in high schools, adult schools, universities, students are amazed. "I thought I hated poetry," they say. "But this is great." The other stuff, the "tepid, mannered, and opaque," stands revealed for what it is. And the fears and antipathies that made people shun poetry disappear.

Once exposed to this kind of clear and lively poetry, no open-minded reader can dismiss all poetry as boring and irrelevant. The poet will once more fill a vital function in our culture. And poetry will have its audience again.

---

80 Kowit, *The Maverick Poets*.
81 Charles Harper Webb, ed., *Stand Up Poetry: An Expanded Anthology* (Iowa City: University of Iowa Press, 2002).

Depression and American Poetry:
A Psychotherapeutic Approach

In Yogi Berra's words, "It's déjà vu all over again." After an hour of reading literary mags, another batch of fledgling poets groans, "Everything's so *down!*"[82]

I know that part of their dismay comes from confronting the hard facts of life expressed by serious poetry. But I don't think that's the whole story—or even most of it.

As an experiment, I pulled a prestigious recent anthology from my bookshelf, read ten poems at random, and noted what they were about.

1. A loved one has died; the speaker's mourning encompasses the poor and downtrodden everywhere.
2. A woman sees her own face contorted with pleasure, and finds it repellant.
3. A man sees the man he used to be disappear as he grows old.
4. A woman dares to speak about some dark secret, probably a molestation.
5. A dog mutilated by its owner waits to die.
6. A boy struggles to express himself, but finally dies.
7. A speaker stares at a winter landscape, feeling empty and depressed.
8. A speaker celebrates nature's abundance, and wants more.
9. A man in prison fights to survive.
10. A speaker describes and decries the horrors of World War II, the Holocaust, and genocide.

---

82 William Greenway notes the same phenomenon. "My graduate course in modern British poetry recently asked me ... why modern poetry was so depressing. Indeed, almost every class I teach asks the same question." William Greenway, "Hoping It Might Be So: Thomas Hardy and the Poetry of Gloom," *ELF: Eclectic Literary Forum* 7, no. 4 (1997–1998).

These summaries don't, of course, do justice to the poems. But I think most psychotherapists would assess the moods of the poems as I did: eight depressive, one non-depressive, one half-and-half. Eighty-five percent depressive.

If this number is close to typical, it's no wonder that my students groan, and that so many readers—especially those who aren't depressive, and don't want to be—avoid poetry. A great depressive poem may seize our interest and exalt our spirits as it breaks our hearts. It may provide much-needed catharsis. But few poems, depressive or otherwise, are great. The mediocre depressive poem is, almost by definition, depressing and dull.[83] That combination is, for most readers, the kiss of death: a kiss for which American poetry has been puckering for a long time.

Most people who've written poems wrote their first when unhappy. Many poets, though, continue to draw most or all of their inspiration from that painful state. Happy people, if they can, tend to keep doing what has made them happy. Sadness, though, seems to call out for artistic expression. Fully expressing one's unhappiness helps to distance from it, and gives a sense of power over it.

The relief experienced by expressing inner pain is at the heart of the psychotherapeutic process and, as Louise Glück details in her essay "Fear of Happiness,"[84] is often at the heart of the artistic process too. Glück describes how some writers become addicted to the catharsis that writing can provide. Dependant on feelings of self-worth derived from being a writer, they may keep themselves unhappy, and their lives static and stuck, in order to nourish the pain they think essential to their art. Small wonder if their work seems stuck: limited in scope, and always sad.

Worse, as their pain increases, its power to inspire diminishes, giving rise to "an art hardly deserving of that name, an art too predictable in its judgments and, finally, too superficial to attract attention over time."[85]

If this dynamic is true for many poets, it's not surprising that contemporary American poetry as a whole feels, in the language of clinical psychology, *dysthymic*.[86]

The *Diagnostic and Statistical Manual of Mental Disorders IV* defines *dysthymia* (sometimes called *depressive neurosis*) as a depressed mood "for

---

83 Dulled affect is a hallmark of depression.

84 Louise Glück, "Fear of Happiness," *Michigan Quarterly Review* XXV, no. 4 (1996).

85 Glück, "Fear of Happiness," 584.

86 Major (also called "clinical") depression—as opposed to dysthymia—is unhappiness so severe as to make the word "unhappy" seem inadequate. While in the throes of major depression, people don't write poetry.

most of the day, more days than not." Since, taken as a whole, American Poetry exhibits a depressed mood for most of any given book or magazine, more of the time than not, I think the diagnosis fits.

For an individual to be labeled dysthymic/depressive, the *DSM IV* states that he or she must experience at least two of the following chronic symptoms: 1. poor appetite or overeating, 2. insomnia or hypersomnia, 3. low energy or fatigue, 4. low self-esteem, 5. poor concentration or difficulty making decisions, 6. feelings of hopelessness.

These symptoms can also be diagnostic for poems.

Much of T. S. Eliot's work,[87] for instance, is prototypically depressive. His best-known poetry is marked by a sense of enervation, loss, and despair. J. Alfred Prufrock shows classic symptoms of dysthymia: low self-esteem, low energy, difficulty making decisions, feelings of hopelessness.[88] As for *The Waste Land*—the title says it all.

William Carlos Williams's best-known poems, by contrast, are celebrations: the delicious plums in "This is Just to Say;" the transcendent "red wheel / barrow . . . beside the white / chickens." Even "The Widow's Lament in Springtime" is a celebration of grieving—a luxurious grieving, full of sensual energy. There is no loss of appetite in these three poems, no feeling of world-weary fatigue.

It's no surprise, for those who know her history, that Anne Sexton's poems reveal a deep world-weariness, along with hopelessness and desire for death. In "With Mercy for the Greedy," Sexton's speaker states, "I detest my sins and I try to believe / in The Cross." This one line expresses two symptoms of dysthymia: difficulty making decisions, and low self-esteem.

Frank O'Hara is a horse of a lighter color. "Poem" [Lana Turner has collapsed . . .][89] is confident, breezy, witty, irreverent, yet also tender and touching. The speaker admits to acting "perfectly disgraceful" at parties, but there is no sense that he feels bad about himself or his grammar. Rather, he seems proud of both. Not only is "Poem" not hopeless, it bubbles with good-humored optimism. All one has to do upon collapsing—especially if one is Lana Turner, universally adored—is just "get up."

In a sense, the act of writing a poem—even a despairing one—is an optimistic act. For the most part, though, depressive poems present a pessimistic outlook. The best may possess somber gravity, a sense of weight

---

87 I'm diagnosing poems, not poets.

88 If I were treating him, I would expect disturbances of appetite and sleeping too.

89 Frank O'Hara, *Lunch Poems* (San Francisco: City Lights Books, 1964).

and depth, a profound understanding of sorrow, suffering, tragedy. The worst are glum, self-pitying, inert.

Anyone who observes babies knows that, from birth, some are cheerful, outgoing, adventurous, assertive, while others are withdrawn, suspicious, shy, colicky. Psychological and biological evidence suggests that a depressive or non-depressive outlook is the product, not of insight and intelligence, but of *temperament*: the result of complex interactions between inborn emotional predispositions and the experiences of infancy and early childhood. Depending on their temperaments, people may respond to the same event—rape, war, falling in love—quite differently, and write very different poems about it.

A friend whom I'll call X insists that the often-celebrated "happy childhood" is a myth, and that "Fern Hill" was either the product of repression, or a lie. As proof he notes that Dylan Thomas drank himself to death.

Not surprisingly, X writes mainly depressive poems. His intelligence and sense of humor keep him from getting stuck in the way that Glück describes. He writes well—but not as well, I think, as he would if his psyche were more open to the possibility of happiness.

Studies suggest that pessimists have a more accurate picture of the world than optimists. Optimists, on the other hand, seem to be more effective in the world. In the area of Art, depressive and non-depressive outlooks—the glass half empty, or the glass half full—can be considered equally valid.

Dylan Thomas emptied many a glass, and bottle too. I don't know how he viewed their fullness, or why he drank. I do know "Fern Hill" is a non-depressive poem, full of energy and high spirits—sensual, playful, celebrative, although propelled by a tragic vision of mortality. Non-depressives also recognize life's sorrows, and may write about them with passion and profundity.

Yet many poets and critics devalue non-depressive art. Kenneth Koch states, "Some readers think of a poem as a sort of ceremony—a funeral, a wedding—where anything 'comic' is out of order. . . . Dissociation, even obscurity, may be tolerated, but only as long as the tone remains solemn or sad enough."[90]

The prejudice in favor of depressive art goes back at least as far as Aristotle, who proclaimed Tragedy superior to Comedy.[91] To this day, it is

---

90 Kenneth Koch, interview by Jordan Davis, *American Poetry Review* XXV, no. 6 (1996).

91 Tragedy is not universally depressive. Hamlet was depressed; *Hamlet* is not. Neither is Comedy always non-depressive. Look at *Waiting for Godot*.

widely assumed—though sometimes unconsciously—that an optimistic, non-depressive outlook is, *a priori*, less "deep" than a depressive one.

Good psychotherapists know that this is nonsense. Any reasonably bright child of ten can see that many things in life—including death—are cruel, unjust, and far more painful, vicious, and depressing than parents or culture readily admit. It shows no more depth of character to slouch through life depressed, like the archetypal alienated adolescent, than to skip through life oblivious. The greatness of a human spirit is determined by the courage, sensitivity, and intelligence with which it faces life, regardless of inborn temperament.

Yet, although depressive and non-depressive poems may have equal value as art, dysthymia is, by definition, pathological. It is painful, and it impairs functioning—which may include the poet's work.

The poor mental health of many writers is well-known. A recent article in *The British Journal of Psychiatry* found psychosis or depression in eighty percent of sampled poets. An earlier study of MFA students at the University of Iowa revealed a high incidence of psychopathology, with depression in the lead. As poetry becomes more a profession and less a calling, those drawn to it seem to be veering away from the more florid psychopathologies, and toward dysthymia. Many poets now strike me as sad accountants whose medium is words—weary middle-managers less concerned with writing astonishing poems than with pleasing the powers that portion out prizes and jobs. These careful, conscientious conformists are ideally suited to produce the well-crafted but low-energy, low-risk, often dysthymic "McPoem."[92]

I sense, too, a disingenuousness in many depressive poems—a groping for moral authority based on suffering. This at least partially explains why so many contemporary poems deal with oppressed and tortured people from another place or time. Instead of compassionate and humane, as these "socially aware" poems are meant to be, many strike me as preachy, peevish, and preening. "Face it," they seem to say. "You're only moral if you feel as I do. And, since I wrote this, I'm more moral than you."

Though most of us may wish that we were younger, richer, taller, prettier, more famous, or had "a steady job and no worry about the future,"[93] by comparison to most people in the world, the least successful poet in the

---

92 This felicitous term was coined by Donald Hall in his famous essay "Poetry and Ambition."
93 Ezra Pound, "Further Instructions" in *The New Poetry: An Anthology*, ed. Harriet Monroe, Alice Henderson (New York: Macmillan, 1917).

United States is a king. The melancholy of many American poets smacks of neurosis and narcissism. It rings hollow—unlike, for instance, the mood of Eastern European poets, who, despite or because of what they've suffered, seem less melancholy than Americans, and know themselves to be vastly better off than, for instance, the average Rwandan.

Sometimes I want to yell at American poets, "Stop sniveling! There's no need to pretend to be less happy than you are—or to be more unhappy than you have to be." More than one poet has abused drugs or alcohol because a poet s/he admired did, and s/he thought such abuse might be the royal road to poetry.

Now that is sad! Americans have the luxury of writing about subjects of which our ancestors could not conceive. We have the chance to depict, dissect, criticize, and celebrate a way of life and a body of knowledge that humankind has never experienced before. As Louise Glück's therapist told her, "The world . . . will provide you sorrow enough."[94] There's no point trying to make more.

Yet despite our opportunities and advantages, despite the abundant talent our poets possess, American poetry's dysthymia flourishes.

Given the fact of human mortality, good art may always contain more sadness than would be "healthy" for an individual. But an eighty-five/fifteen split is just too high.

Excluding other poets and student-conscripts, the audience for American poetry is small, and seems, in my experience, to consist mainly of people who are either depressive themselves and like to see their worldview validated, or those with high tolerance for depressive material.[95] Most people don't. Given one more reason to shun poetry, they do, leaving the depressives to applaud and reward depressive poems, causing more to be written, and fueling the vicious circle that has rolled poetry to the margins of our culture.

Denied NEA funding for the nth time, one exuberantly non-depressive poet—call her Y—found among the judges' comments on her work, "Enthusiasm should be tempered." Who but a depressive criticizes in that way?

---

94 Louise Glück, "Fear of Happiness," 580.

95 William Greenway notes, only half-jokingly, that he may prefer depressive poems because he's depressive himself. Greenway, "Hoping It Might Be So: Thomas Hardy and the Poetry of Gloom."

If a patient comes to me reporting eighty-five percent depressive thoughts, I can be sure s/he needs serious help. So here, gratis, are my therapeutic suggestions for U.S. poetry.

1. Poets—don't stop writing depressive poems

You must be true to your vision, or your poems will be worthless. It is possible, though, to widen that vision, and to write from that expanded outlook. Louise Glück describes how psychotherapy helped her to accept more happiness into her life. By doing this, she found that "What unhappiness tends to perpetuate is an isolating and, usually, limitless fixation on the self; except in the rarest cases, this is bound to be an aesthetic limitation. Whereas . . . Happiness surprises . . . it releases information"[96]—and, sometimes, new and better poetry.

If you write mainly from negative states, try this: For every depressive poem you write—or every two—write an optimistic/celebrative one. Welcome wit and humor into your poems. Learn to use it as deftly as you use more somber elements. Even if the resulting work is not your best—even if you never publish it—the influence on your other poems will be salutary.

2. The prejudice in favor of depressive poems must end

When a non-depressive idea rears its head, many poets shoo it away. "I can't write poetry about that!" This position limits the scope of their work, and may also keep their lives needlessly sad.

Equally bad—when poets do write from a non-depressive state, editors frown. Another poet—Z[97]—told me, "I'd love to write more poems with humor and élan. But when I do, I don't get anywhere with them. Not even 'Sorry' on the rejection slip."

Some editors need an infusion of happiness, too.

I'm struck by the way, at readings, certain poets intersperse depressive poems with witty comments, or even comedy routines. Charles Baxter describes poets at parties as the ones "who are usually having a fine time in the center of the spotlight, making a spectacle of themselves."[98] If those

---

96 Louise Glück, "Fear of Happiness," 585.

97 My poet-witnesses' unwillingness to criticize the status quo on the record speaks volumes about the poetry "scene," where material success depends so little on the response of general readers—because there are so few—and so much on the good will of other members of the scene.

98 Charles Baxter, "Rhyming Action," *Michigan Quarterly Review* XXV, no. 4 (1996): 617.

poets used that livelier, funnier, wilder side of themselves in their work, poetry and readers would be the richer for it.

One of the many reasons we venerate Shakespeare is his amazing breadth: tragedy one minute, farce the next. Isn't that more true-to-life and emotionally compelling, not to mention more entertaining and psychologically healthier, than unrelenting gloom? Or unrelenting gaiety? Isn't breadth a goal toward which most poets might aspire?

There has been, lately, a strong push to open the Western Canon to underrepresented minorities. How about opening it to another underrepresented minority: the Non-Depressive? Richard Garcia says of James Tate, "Reading him just gets me into a good mood." Couldn't American poetry use more poets whose work does that? Billy Collins, Barbara Hamby, Thomas Lux, Denise Duhamel, Ron Koertge, Pattianne Rogers, and Albert Goldbarth are among those making inroads. Kenneth Koch has been leading his own idiosyncratic charge for years. But the depressive/non-depressive scale still tilts precipitously Down.

American poets have been out of the public eye so long that many have made a virtue of it. Still, I'm convinced that most poets would welcome a larger, more appreciative audience. I'm equally convinced that they could have it if American poetry achieved a better depressive/non-depressive ratio.

I want to stress that, when I speak of non-depressive poetry, I don't mean *Polyanna's Collected Homilies*. I mean poems with verve, energy, deep feeling—even pain and heartbreak—but not written out of despair.

Albert Goldbarth's poem "Life is Happy"[99] has a horrifying central image of a zebra disemboweled by a lion. ". . . that zebra's widened jaws / and splayed gray teeth would bray inside my brain / for years . . .," the poet states. But he goes on to show that, despite abundant suffering and horror in individual lives, the nature of Life is to be joyous. Life is itself an expression of happiness.

Without detracting from sad poetry, let's raise the status and frequency of the happier kind. Let's give wit, energy, humor, and enthusiasm the praise they're due. Let's esteem celebration as highly as lamentation, rhapsody as much as elegy. Let's recognize that examined optimism is a philosophically advanced position, harder to achieve and fully as honorable as examined pessimism, and much more advanced than adolescent gloom, however sophisticated its expression.

---

99 Albert Goldbarth, *Marriage and Other Science Fiction* (Columbus: Ohio State University Press, 1994).

The goal of Jungian psychotherapy is to achieve balance, exemplified by the possession of a wide range of possible responses and behaviors. Such psychological balance makes the possessor more effective in life, happier, and more fulfilled. As a poet, a reader, and a psychotherapist, I wish that healthy state for American Poetry.

The Pleasure of Their Company:
Voice and Poetry

Beginning poets who interpret criticism of their poems as criticism of themselves are onto something. However loudly we proclaim the poem to be separate from the poet, people respond to poems *as if* they are real people speaking. New Critics and post-structuralists, unreliable narrators, personae, slipping signifiers, and self-deconstructing "I"s notwithstanding, this is true. The poetical is personal.

A good poem speaks in a voice I like to hear. Though not entirely unfamiliar, the voice is not one that I've heard before. It inspires confidence. It demands and rewards attention, offering entry into a psyche that intrigues, and may delight.

T. S. Eliot was wrong to declare poetry "not the expression of personality but an escape from personality."[100] It's true that the speaker of a poem by X is not identical to the X who orders chicken-with-chef's-special-sauce at Panda Inn. It's also true that many bad poems lean too heavily on personality. Yet where can poems come from, if not the poet's personality? Poetry does not spring, full-blown, from Language's side—despite theorists who seem to think that their own wind will breathe life into their inanimate god. To play Hamlet effectively, an actor must locate the part of himself that resonates with Hamlet. Similarly, a good poet writes from that part of his/her personality able to inhabit the speaker of the poem.

No poem can express the poet's entire personality; still, a good poem conveys a fair-sized chunk. The poet's *voice* is that chunk, expressed on the page.

The most learned among us has not spent more than a few decades studying literature. Our ancestors, though, spent hundreds of millennia evolving the ability to size up their own kind, sensing whether to like them,

---

100 T. S. Eliot, "Tradition and the Individual Talent," in *The Sacred Wood*, (London: Metheum Publishers, 1920).

trust them, hate them, follow them. Hominids who could not accurately assess the character, intentions, and competence of their fellows carried a big handicap into Evolution's games. Their genes likely did not survive.

Poet Louis Simpson states, "I cannot explain my aversion to [James Merrill's] style except as an aversion to the personality it presents. The style is the man."[101]

Interesting, likable (or unlikable in an interesting way), insightful, bright, truthful, pompous, preening, muddle-headed, dull—all of these qualities and more are conveyed through a poet's voice. People evolved to respond favorably to certain voices—to accept the voices' owners as leaders, experts, or in any case, worth listening to. The success and proliferation of dull poetry is at least partly due to the tendency to second-guess and override one's "gut" response to voice.[102]

Poems that I like are spoken by voices that compel my attention in some pleasing, primal way. I enjoy the poems', and by extension, the poets' company—on the page, at any rate. If T. S. Eliot's personality did not come through in his poems—if he lacked, that is, a compelling voice—no one would care what he thought about poetry. To speak as powerfully as Eliot's poems do to readers who can't know him personally, the poet's voice must be compelling, and it must be unique.

The voice may shift as a writer changes points of view, and *must* shift somewhat as the writer ages; yet, since personality is quite stable after age five, a good poet's voice—however wide-ranging—stays recognizably his or her own. Robert Lowell's style shifted substantially between *Lord Weary's Castle* and *Life Studies*. The controlling personality—and therefore, at deep levels, the voice—stayed much the same.[103]

Gray hair and decades of practice notwithstanding, the poet who lacks a unique and compelling voice remains a novice. Yet, though every person has a unique, potentially compelling history and genetic makeup, such voices are rare. This is partly due to a lack of what we might as well call talent, and partly due to restrictions caused by socialization. The overly

---

101 Louis Simpson, "Reflections on Narrative Poetry," in *A Company of Poets* (Ann Arbor: University of Michigan Press, 1981): 346–55.

102 Increased suppression by the rational mind of this and other intuitive responses by the rational mind is a mark of the educated person. It also helps to explain the lack of "common sense" of which intellectuals are frequently accused.

103 Though Fernando Pessoa's *noms de plume* can be considered different people, each with a different voice, it makes more psychological sense to consider them the work of one man who, like Shakespeare and Whitman, contained "multitudes."

socialized voice may sound sophisticated, kind, efficient, even charming, but it is rarely compelling, never unique, and always hollow.

A poet's voice may be said to consist of four major, mutually influencing components:

1. Diction

Diction includes vocabulary, rhythm, cadence, and characteristic patterns of syntax. Tony Hoagland's diction is pungent, down-to-earth, colloquial. Amy Gerstler's, as well as being colloquial, is quirky, anxious, strange. T. S. Eliot's is formal, learned, vatic, with colloquial snippets thrown in.

Most people mean diction when they speak of a writer's "style."

2. Subject Matter

Does the poet favor romance? Sexual intrigue? Power struggles? Big game hunting? Children? Politics? What are his or her passions and obsessions?

A poet's subject matter also includes, and depends on, the memory pool that provides his or her imagery. David Kirby's memory pool is full of scenes from a suburban childhood in the South. Wanda Coleman's is full of South-Central LA.

Since everyone's personal history is unique, the poet who effectively taps his/her memory pool is well on the way to a unique voice.

3. Temperament

Temperament—much of it genetically based[104]—shapes the poet's worldview, helping to determine whether he/she is misanthrope or philanthrope, optimist or pessimist, wiseacre or stern moralist. It influences, too, the poet's choice of forms, since aesthetics rise from temperament.

Barbara Hamby's poems seem optimistic, though with their ballast of mortality, they are in no danger of floating off the page. Mark Strand's work is darker and more pessimistic.

Whatever the poet's temperament, the poems reflect it.

---

104 Psychologist Steven Pinker lists five major ways in which temperament varies genetically: openness to experience, conscientiousness, extroversion-introversion, antagonism-agreeableness, and neuroticism. Steven Pinker, *The Blank Slate: the Modern Denial of Human Nature* (New York: Viking, 2002): 375.

4. Style of thought

Style of thought[105] concerns the workings of the poet's mind. This includes the quality of thoughts—their incisiveness, originality, cogency, lyricism, emotional charge, and general aesthetic thrust.

Does the poet proceed by intuitive leaps, as Dean Young often does, or more logically and scientifically, like Lynn Emanuel? Does he or she favor realism or flights of fancy, the sledgehammer or the rapier? What does the play of the poet's consciousness look like? And how about the unconscious?

As every human voice creates a unique pattern on an oscilloscope, so every mind shows a unique pattern of thought—the more unique the mind, the more unique, potentially, the voice.

What About Imagination?

Clearly, good writing need not come directly from the writer's personal experience. Stephen Crane did not fight in the Civil War, yet *The Red Badge of Courage* is as convincing as any firsthand account. Still, Eliot is wrong to declare, ". . . emotions which he [the author] has never experienced will serve his turn as well as those familiar to him."[106] Imagination can seem godlike in its ability to extrapolate, embellish, generalize; but it does not create out of a void. Crane knew well the emotions he depicts.

A boy whose pet turtle is crushed by a truck may grow up to write movingly about death and loss. But a writer with no experience of passionate sexual love could no more write *Romeo and Juliet* than a person deaf from birth could write Beethoven's *Fifth*.

Eliot contends that ". . . the poet has, not a 'personality' to express, but a particular medium, which is only the medium and not the personality, in which impressions and experiences combine in peculiar and unexpected ways. Impressions and experiences that are important for the man may take no place in the poetry, and those that become important in the poetry may play quite a negligible part in the man, the personality."[107]

This approaches Barthes's poststructuralist notion that authors do not create, but only "draw upon that immense dictionary of language and cul-

---

105 Louise Glück equates this with voice itself. "The poem will not survive on content but through voice," she states in an interview. "By voice I mean the style of thought, for which a style of speech never convincingly substitutes."

106 Eliot, *The Sacred Wood*.

107 Eliot, *The Sacred Wood*.

ture which is 'always already written.'"[108] This is an interesting notion, but unsupported by empirical evidence. While experimental writers may bypass the personality, generating text by purely mechanical manipulations, few people would rank those productions beside the best of Shakespeare, or even Danielle Steele.[109]

Writing is not the act of a language or medium arranging itself into permutations. It is a purposeful act, driven by volition, which arises out of personality. Every successful liar knows that the more truth a lie contains, the more believable it is. A poet who is cruel in private life can write convincing poems of kindness and compassion by drawing on the kindness and compassion that coexist with cruelty in his/her personality.

To play King Lear requires an older actor, not so much for the physical attributes of age, but for the years of experience needed to undergird the role, supporting it as breath supports the singing voice. Musical prodigies amaze with early virtuosity, but most require more living-time to play with conviction and emotional maturity.

Failures of Voice

Failures of voice may be due to problems with talent, craft, self-censorship, personality, or some combination of the four.

The poet with *insufficient talent*[110] is like a center fielder who lacks the reflexes to chase down a fly ball or hit a curve. No amount of practice will get that player to the major leagues; and no amount of writing will give that poet a unique, compelling voice.

Problems with craft are helped by practice. Still, just as few violinists become expert enough for the concert stage, few poets develop enough craft to write masterful poems. Failing to feel a compelling *author*ity in the voice, readers distrust and reject the poems.

Problems of self-censorship occur when the writer has talent and a unique, compelling personality, but these qualities don't reach the page. More than one poet whose voice is lively and engaging in conversation, lapses into dull anonymity when the poems begin.

---

108 Raman Selden, Peter Widdowson, and Peter Brooker, *A Reader's Guide to Contemporary Literary Theory*, 4th ed. (Longman, 1997): 66.

109 T. S. Eliot's own personality leaps out of his work, even as he denies the importance of personality. "But of course, only those who have personality and emotions know what it means to want to escape from these things," he writes—speaking, I'm sure, about himself. Eliot, *The Sacred Wood*.

110 Many aspects of what we call *talent* can be learned; but no one can learn to write as well as Shakespeare.

This problem—as if a V8 engine were running on four cylinders—is often due to a limiting concept of poetry. For Billy Collins to change from a self-described writer of "bad imitations" into one of the more original voices in U.S. poetry, he had "to allow into my poetry aspects of my self—my sensibility and my experience—that I had been unwittingly censoring."[111]

The self-censoring poet may feel, as Collins did, that humor is inappropriate in poems. He or she may believe that only certain subjects and moral positions lend themselves to poetry. Such problems may be corrected by a shift in attitude (though the shift may take years). If the shift is consistently resisted, the problem may lie with the personality.

By *problems of personality*, I don't mean the ones that drive people into psychotherapy—anxiety, depression, difficulty bonding, etc. Nor do I mean the poet is "mentally ill." The problems to which I refer are qualities of personality that keep the poet from doing his or her best work. Psychological blind spots—for instance, lack of insight into other people—show up as blind spots in poetry. A man's unresolved anger toward women may show itself in poorly drawn, stereotyped female characters. Areas of blocked emotion give rise to emotionally flat poems. Psychic regions the poet has explored insufficiently—sex, violence, anger, grief—reveal themselves in a lack of clarity and penetration, or in reliance on conventional thinking and cliché. Even problems with overeating may manifest in wordy poems, and difficulty in trimming them down.[112]

To fix these problems, psychological restrictions[113] must be loosened, allowing the personality to develop and express itself more fully. The writer may become his or her own psychotherapist, or may pay for the service. In either case, the goal of therapy is not to alleviate external symptoms—these may, in fact, provide good material for poems—but to increase self-awareness and options for expression. Good poets may be cruel, egotistical, sociopathic. They may be neurotic, or even psychotic. But they must be able to see clearly from their highly personal perspective, and to tell the truth of what they see. Failure to do either of these things will cause the reader to distrust and/or dislike, not the "speaker," but the poet.

Moralizers will sound pompous and fraudulent with their insights and epiphanies, more interested in looking admirable than in offering an authentic "take" on the world.

---

111 Billy Collins, "The End of Boredom," *New Letters*, Winter (2004): 155.

112 These examples come straight from my private practice as a psychotherapist.

113 Restrictions caused by temperament or other biological factors constitute failure of talent.

Poets whose main concern is pleasing the cognoscenti will write in styles and about subjects that they think will find critical favor. Their poems will be forms of social one-upsmanship.

Poets who fear self-exposure will write falsely or obscurely. Those who fear being silly will write poems devoid of playfulness or fun. Grown-up teachers' pets will grind out bloodless, proper poems that merit A+ for effort, and C for everything else.

Poets too impressed by what has been written before will repeat it in inferior form. Poets who hate the past too much will write nothing that lasts.

Poets unsure of the value of their perceptions may write timid, waffling poems full of self-defeating contradictions, or may disguise their timidity with obscurantism and gratuitous strangeness.

Poets who fear that they are not original will write poems that strain. Poets with a need to pose will write poems of empty attitude. Poets writing just to write will write inconsequentially. Poets who want to be shamans will sound like quacks. Poets too proud of being poets will write every poem in praise of themselves.

Only the deluded, the masochistic, and students under duress will read more than a little of such poetry.

Qualities of a Compelling Voice

A good poem, like a good friend, is a pleasure to be with. It has special talents, amazing abilities, yet meets the reader as an equal. It does not flatter or condescend. It illuminates, encourages, entertains, and does not bore.

To write such a poem requires talent, mastery of craft, minimal self-censorship, and a unique, compelling personality. The personality must be risk-taking, adventurous, and confident (at least in the mental sphere). It must be rebellious, dissatisfied with received wisdom and the status quo.[114] It must be strongly emotional, as well as highly intelligent, imaginative, and original. If the personality has these qualities, the voice will possess three qualities central to good poetry: wit, passion, and impropriety.

---

114 "Society depends on the poet to witness something, and yet the poet can discover that thing only by looking away from what society has learned to see poetically." Robert Pinsky, "Responsibilities of the Poet," in *Poetry and the World* (New York: Ecco Press, 1988): 83–98.

1. Wit

The importance to poetry of wit—meaning *quickness of perception, ingenuity, keen intelligence*—is self-evident. A poet who lacks this kind of wit will evince a low quality of thought.

Wit meaning *humor* can be important too. People who lack a sense of humor may, on first meeting, seem "nice"—even exceptionally so; but frequently, they pall. Nothing about them strikes sparks. Nothing seems fun. The imaginative leaps and unexpected connections characteristic of a first-rate mind may be absent. The sense of common humanity and the general uplift that laughter can provide are absent in the humorless person's conversation and poems.

2. Passion

Passionate writing makes the reader deal with strong emotion. This is risky in a culture embarrassed by emotion, and even riskier when judgments about poems are made by critics and theorists who, with no firsthand knowledge of the passions and wild enthusiasms of real scientists, cultivate what they think is scientific objectivity.

To admit passion into poetry, as to admit love into one's life, is to risk being judged excessive, undiscriminating, jejune, ridiculous—especially if that passion is high-spirited and celebratory. To avoid such judgments, some poets cultivate understatement, obliqueness, and dour depressiveness. They proceed by indirection, fearing to call a spade a spade and be told, "No, fool, that is a club."

How dreary, though, to speak with someone who lacks passion. Like humorless people, the passionless may seem agreeable at first. But how "connect" with someone who is barely there? Eventually, we give up and go away.

3. Impropriety

Civilization is designed to shield people from, among other things, unsettling truths. Biology being what it is, some aspects of human life are sure to distress our "higher" consciousness. In addition, since power seeks to maintain itself, lies spring up to support the status quo.

Standards of propriety help to keep unpleasant, upsetting, dangerous realities out of mind. Politeness, which means suppressing anything that could make anyone uncomfortable, rules out much humor and most passion.

Employed for its own sake, impropriety is almost as uninteresting as strict propriety. However, since many truths are improper, indecorous, or uncomfortable, a person who avoids impropriety must also avoid truth. The proper person, like the humorless and the passionless, will be dull. To escape controversy, such a person must censor imagination (who can tell where it will lead?), avoid penetrating insights (always potentially shocking), and keep excitement controlled (lest all hell break loose). Such a poet may create pretty pictures and artfullydisguised homilies, but not compelling art.

Voices I Like to Hear

MRI studies of people making difficult decisions reveal that, though the subjects think they're being rational, they decide based primarily on emotion, then think of reasons why their decisions make sense. Similarly, readers of poetry may present complex and lengthy rationales to justify judgments based largely on emotional responses to the poet's voice.

In "Dawn Walk," Edward Hirsch expresses compassion, tenderness, and love.

> Some nights when you're asleep
> Deep under the covers, far away,
> Slowly curling yourself back
> Into a childhood no one
> Living will ever remember
> Now that your parents touch hands
> Under the ground
> As they always did upstairs
> In the master bedroom . . .

The personality behind this voice seems modest, grateful, honest, and vulnerable.

> . . . Cars,
> Too, are rimmed and motionless
> Under a thin blanket smoothed down
> By the smooth maternal palm
> Of the wind. So thanks to the
> Blue morning, to the blue spirit

> Of winter, to the soothing blue gift
> Of powdered snow![115]

Through apt metaphors, the voice conveys intelligence and careful observation. It speaks gently, as if to soothe loved ones to sleep. It is anxious, but the anxiety is reasonable, born of the fear of losing those the speaker loves.

The voice is not neurotically fretful and self-involved. Nor, for all its gentleness, is it sentimental or epicene. It is not affected; it does not show off. Rather, it seems to speak truthfully about the speaker's emotions. Since those emotions and the sensibility behind them feel close to my own, it's not surprising that I find the poem moving and beautiful.

Where Hirsch's poem is realistic and domestic, the voice of Brigit Pegeen Kelly in "Song" is eerie, mythic, and wild.

> Listen: there was a goat's head hanging by ropes in a tree.
> All night it hung there and sang. And those who heard it
> Felt a hurt in their hearts and thought they were hearing
> The song of a night bird . . .

Kelly's voice is shamanic, telling tales about a world of violence and sorrow, of tenderness and forgiveness, but also of punishment.

> The goat cried like a man and struggled hard. But they
> Finished the job. They hung the bleeding head by the school
> And then ran off into the darkness that seems to hide everything
>   . . . What they didn't know
> Was that the goat's head would go on singing, just for them,
>   . . . They would
> Wake in the night thinking they heard the wind in the trees
> Or a night bird, but their hearts beating harder. There
> Would be a whistle, a hum, a high murmur, and, at last, a song,
> The low song a lost boy sings remembering his mother's call.
> Not a cruel song, no, no, not cruel at all. This song
> Is sweet. It is sweet. The heart dies of this sweetness.[116]

---

115 Edward Hirsch, *Wild Gratitude* (New York: Knopf, 1990): 77.
116 Brigit Pegeen Kelly, *Song* (Rochester: BOA Editions, 1995): 15.

Kelly tells her story with passion and verve, without affectation. I find myself pulled into her mythic world, moved by its horror and beauty. The personality that her voice conveys feels different enough from mine to intrigue, but close enough not to exclude me. Her voice carries the fascination of the exotic, allowing me to experience her primal and compelling poetry.

James Tate is not a poet at all, some say; others claim that he's among our best. Certainly, the voice in "To Each His Own" [117] conveys a personality either unconcerned with poetic convention, or actively mocking it.

The sonnet-length poem tells how a man named Joey came back from "the war" with "a tattoo on his right hand that said DEVI," and "wouldn't even tell what that meant." He spent his spare time working on his "Indian motorcycle" until it "ran like a top. It gleamed. It purred." Then ". . . One night at dinner / he shocked us all by saying, 'Devi's coming to / live with us. It's going to be difficult. She's / an elephant.'"

The language here is casual, chatty, even childish. There's little concrete imagery. Lines show no metrical regularity and, ranging from nine to fourteen syllables, seem broken with no purpose but to make them roughly the same length on the page. "Prose broken into lines," critics could easily say.

Yet Tate's voice strikes me as poetically sophisticated in its very unpoeticness. The text contains only one simile, and that is a cliché; yet the whole poem is an effective metaphor. Joey, who loves an elephant, could be any star-crossed lover, whether a Montague pining for his Capulet, or a gay man coming out. Tate's voice does not convey noble feeling and high seriousness. The consciousness at work in this poem evokes sympathy for Joey and Devi, even as it makes fun of the whole affair.

Tate's voice conveys a wild and uninhibited imagination, and an unabashed silliness that resonates with the most fun-loving part of me. Someone else might find the voice flat, the poem ridiculous. I find both voice and poem refreshing, entertaining, and curative. When I feel mentally waterlogged, Tate throws me a lifeline.

Sharon Olds, as controversial as Tate, has been lauded and pilloried for her willingness to go where few poets have gone before. In "The Unjustly Punished Child," [118] she uses vivid metaphors to express an unvarnished truth about injustice.

---

117 James Tate, *Memoir of the Hawk* (New York: Ecco Press, 2001),:72.
118 Sharon Olds, *Satan Says* (Pittsburgh: University of Pittsburgh Press, 1980): 55.

The child screams in his room. Rage
heats his head.
He is going through changes like metal under deep
pressure at high temperatures.

When he cools off and comes out of that door
he will not be the same child who ran in
and slammed it. An alloy has been added. Now he will
crack along different lines when tapped.

He is stronger. The long impurification
has begun this morning.

This short poem strikes me as brave, hard-hitting, thought-provoking, passionately felt, and absolutely true. I love the strength of the voice, its sense of clarity, authority, compassion, and unapologetic wisdom. The speaker seems a person whose company I would seek out. It's no wonder that I admire this poem.

Conclusion

Walt Whitman states in his journal, "There is no trick or cunning, no art or recipe, by which you can have in your writing what you do not possess in yourself." If this is true, as I believe it is, the only way to write with a unique and compelling voice is to have—or develop—a unique, compelling personality.

The best poets never cease to work at this. Whether they aim, like Shakespeare, to broaden their consciousness or, like Philip Larkin, to stake out a limited terrain and dig deep, these poets learn to observe carefully the outside world, as well as the inner, psychic one. They continue to experiment and try new things—maybe not in their lives, but always in their art. They don't stagnate. They strive to learn the truth and tell it, however idiosyncratic and time-limited it may be.

Good poets don't need to root out and "cure" character flaws, but must be willing to explore fully and honestly those they have. The best poets may be liars, but their poems don't lie. The best poets may not live wisely, but they are wise in their poetry. The best poets must be narcissistic enough to think their words important, but not so narcissistic as to think *all* their words are. Good poets may love their own poetry, but must love Poetry more.

Should a poet achieve a unique, compelling voice along with critical acclaim, he or she must battle with success from that time on. Convinced of their own genius by prizes and reviews, some poets start to go easy on themselves. When this happens, craft deteriorates. The voice sounds self-indulgent and self-involved—because it is.

Success leads naturally to a wish for more. This can become a need to please that, unchecked, leads to self-censorship and fear of risk—qualities that damage and distort the voice.

The poet must not try to change the voice in hopes of becoming more popular. Even if popularity increases, the voice is compromised; the poems decline.

If Shakespeare's voice resonates with more people than Larkin's, so be it. Both voices are unique, compelling, and valid artistically. Both express what their authors had to give. Decisions concerning greatness versus goodness, major status or minor, are made by readers, change with literary fashions, and are not subject to the author's will.

The poet's job is to discover, develop, and express his or her own voice fully and well. Then let the chips fall.

The Myth of Maturity

The concept of maturity is beloved by critics, whether of human behavior or of art.[119] Music scholars speak of Beethoven's "mature" work; psychologists, parents, and lovers pass judgment on others' "maturity" or its lack as if their meaning were self-evident. Yet this usage of the word is based on a biological analogy that becomes shaky when applied to emotions and behavior, and that disintegrates, applied to art. As commonly used to describe human behavior, the word "mature" means little more than "behavior of which I approve"; "immature," "behavior of which I don't." Similarly, to label art "mature" is to mask a moral judgment as an aesthetic and scientific one. Use of the word falsely invokes the psychological authority of the Parent/Superego, and, more problematic still, presupposes the maturity of the judge.

Biological maturity is in most cases a clearly defined state. An organism is sexually mature when it is able to produce viable offspring. It is physically mature when it achieves its maximum size and strength. To call art "mature" is to assert that it has achieved an analogous state of ripeness and full development. On the surface, this makes sense. We may feel that we know intuitively what is meant. But of what does artistic ripeness consist?

In general, artists must reach a high level of technical skill to create effective art. It seems reasonable to call this skill-level maturity. But it is difficult to quantify the measurement. A surgeon's or a pole-vaulter's skill can be objectively assessed. Closely examined, though, judgments of poetic skill prove to rest heavily on the judge's poetic philosophy—subjective by definition. Joseph Duemer judges Beat poetry a "messy movement,"[120]

---

119 " . . . one of the longer, more ambitious entries [in James Haug's poem] 'The Whitestone Bridge,' intimates a possibility of true maturity." Edward Butscher, "From Places Far and Near," *Poet Lore* 85, no. 3 (1990): 52.

120 Duemer, "The Poetics of Awkwardness," 85.

and characterizes much of the work of poet Charles Bukowski as "bombastic," "artless," and "obvious."[121] These judgments appear to describe a lack of skill. Duemer feels, presumably, that the poets in question should emote less, revise more, think more clearly, cut out excess, use more original imagery, and work with greater subtlety. What are such judgments, however, if not reflections of the critic's sense of what poetry *should be*—a philosophical and, ultimately, moral sense?

This same sense is brought to bear even more strongly when content is being judged. And it is content, not skill-level, on which—consciously or not—most critics judge a poet's level of achievement and maturity. Does the poet arrive at the same understandings of the world, the same aesthetic perceptions and moral values, the same emotional and philosophical truths that the critic holds? This, in practice, is the test of maturity. Critics may pretend that maturity is a virtual force of nature that leaps out at them and judges itself.[122] But this is romantic rationalization. Artistic judgments are subjective by definition—culturally, philosophically, morally, and aesthetically biased. The word "mature" hides that bias. Worse, the poetry Establishment has defined the word so narrowly as to rule out an enormous range of poetic styles, subjects, emotions, attitudes. This definition severely restricts the audience for and the vitality of American poetry today.

Our national Voice-of-the-Parent/Superego Ann Landers has tried to define behavioral maturity.[123] I'm not aware of any essay that does the same for poetic maturity; still, a definition can be inferred from the criticism published by prestigious journals, and the poetry included in prestigious anthologies. First and foremost, mature poetry must be *serious* in the most limited sense. Such poetry is often described as "urgent," "essential," "necessary," as if it arose not out of an impulse to play (to create, as in "play jazz"), but impelled by a dire, intense, and overwhelming need to come into existence and be heard. Not surprisingly, didacticism—though overtly frowned on—crops up often, especially in the work of accepted masters. Flights of fancy—i.e., unbridled imagination—may be tolerated and occasionally praised, but are always suspect, potentially whimsical

---

121 Ibid., 84.

122 "Despite my efforts to hold this manuscript back, however, it kept rising to the top until I had simply to conclude that it is the best, the most mature . . ." Maxine Kumin in a letter to *Poets & Writers* (March/April 1991): 8.

123 Ann Landers, "Reader Seeks a Timely Reminder on Maturity," *Los Angeles Times* (January 4, 1991): E5.

and trifling.[124] Grudging nods may be given to humor if the writer is already accepted as mature, but humor is likely to be seen as glib or callow, the product of a lesser sensibility.

High spirits and fun are, almost by definition, less-than-mature. "Mature" work rarely kids around, and when it does, moves with the stiffness of the classical conductor who adds cha-cha-cha to the end of some obligatory pop piece, just to prove that orchestras are human too. To characterize a work with terms connoting immaturity—"sophomoric," "adolescent," "unsophisticated," "naive," "childish," "infantile"[125]—is to damn it utterly. A cool, detached, knowing, and generally superior stance is prized.[126] A poet can never be too somber, too dour.

Poetry, moreover, is expected to be *work*—both to write and to read. Establishment critics distrust the "smooth and easy."[127] Pleasure is suspect, and to be tolerated, must be in the best Puritan tradition, serious and hard-won. As Paul Hoover points out in his essay on "Moral Poetry,"[128] the preferred tone of Establishment poetry—mature by definition—is elegiac or ecstatic, with elegiac the strong favorite. Ecstasy, when present, must be controlled.

Excess of any kind is discouraged. Even enthusiasm may be frowned upon.[129] A "caring" attitude is applauded, but is generally of the see-how-sensitive-I-am-and-how-deeply-yet-subtly-I-feel variety. A stance of "world-weariness and warning"[130] is valued as proof of the poet's insight and personal depth.

The mature emotional tone is by definition tightly controlled, untainted by sentimentality, the "voice carefully modulated, feelings muted and

---

124 Paul Hoover, "Moral Poetry," *American Book Review* 7, no. 1 (1984): 14.

125 Critic Edward Butscher sprinkles such terms liberally throughout his review of five books in a recent issue of *Poet Lore*. "From Places Far and Near," *Poet Lore* 85, no. 3 (1990): 50–58.

126 Edward Butscher displays the stance he seems to be looking for when he writes of the title poem of James Haug's book *The Stolen Car*, "Some adolescent boys or young men on wheels head out in Huck's wake . . ." With the phrase "in Huck's wake," Butscher shows that he is well aware that what Haug's doing has been done, and done better, long ago. The next sentence continues the superior tone. "Its [the poem's] conclusion . . . helps illustrate the minor joys and real limits of Haug's esthetic." Butscher, "From Places Far and Near," 51–52.

127 Duemer, "The Poetics of Awkwardness," 85.

128 Hoover, "Moral Poetry," 14.

129 A poet who wishes to remain anonymous was told bluntly, regarding her unsuccessful application for a grant from the National Endowment for the Arts, ". . . the enthusiasm should be tempered."

130 Hoover, "Moral Poetry," 14.

unobtrusive."[131] Restraint and understatement are mature; excitement and overstatement aren't. I once saw a respected poet start to sob while reading aloud a poem so detached and abstract I had been half asleep before her tears.

"Bad taste"[132] is a cardinal sin. Mature work normally displays a squeamishness about sex—especially the visceral kind[133]—and deep aversion to excretion and anything else vulgar, unseemly, plebian. The "trendy" is taboo[134]—trendy being anything that smacks of current fashion or partakes of popular culture. Mature work strives at all times to be timeless.

It is scarcely surprising that maturity as defined by the poetry Establishment is closely correlated with that Establishment's values: its collective conscience or Superego. The poetry Establishment consists mainly of middle-class, middle-aged liberal humanists: politically left-leaning, psychologically conservative. Members are, or write as if they are, good boys and girls grown into good adults: studious, well-behaved, appropriate at all times. They may see themselves as rebels, but their poetic rebellions are of the quiet, orderly kind, born of "politically correct" opinions supported by their peers. In poetry, these people always support—and constitute— the status quo.

The result of their definition of maturity is apparent in the United States today: a country in which few people read poetry and fewer still read it for pleasure, in which the *Los Angeles Times* calls poetry an "endangered species,"[135] in which literate, intelligent prose writers shake their heads on learning that I write the stuff, and opine sadly that it's an art whose time is done.

But is *maturity* really as powerful and pernicious as I claim? Drop the word from the critical lexicon, and little would change. But drop the attitudes embodied in the word, and the face of American poetry would be transformed. Maturity, named or implied, is the grail toward which most American poets strive. In the process, they put a major crimp in their po-

---

131 Steve Kowit, "The Present State of American Poetry XII," *The New York Quarterly* 38 (1989): 107–18.

132 "Fortunately, such lapses are rare, if disconcerting in their subversion of our trust in the poet's taste." Butscher, "From Places Far and Near," 52.

133 Women and gay poets seem more willing to be sexual in poetry, perhaps because their excursions are seen as bold, throwing off patriarchal chains, while similar male excursions are likely to be seen as shallow and sexist.

134 "Trendiness intrudes, however . . ." Butscher, "From Places Far and Near," 53.

135 Miles, "Nobody Reads Poetry."

etic invention, forcing their poetry down the same few well-trodden roads, and often reducing it to dull irrelevance.

It's fine for middle-class, liberal humanists to applaud poetry that expresses their values and concerns, or increasingly, the concerns of politically "In" minorities. But what about adolescents? What about young women? Young men? What about poor people? Working class people? Nihilists? Republicans? What about people of any race or socioeconomic status whose values don't conform to middle-class, left-leaning, humanistic views of moral and intellectual respectability?

Every anthropologist knows that different cultures have different value systems. Inevitably, each perceives maturity a different way. So do people in different developmental stages—whether or not they use the word. Childhood, adolescence, young adulthood, middle adulthood, old age (euphemistically called maturity)—each stage has its own values and concerns. A five-year-old's experience of love is different from a fifteen-year-old's, is different from a fifty-year-old's, is different from an eighty-five-year-old's. It is shortsighted to assume that one experience is better-developed and morally superior—i.e., more mature—than the other. The experiences, like the needs felt during those life-stages, are different: grapes and grapefruit, morally non-comparable.

Why, then, should disparate groups all be expected to embrace the same values in poetry? Consider the classic "goody-two shoes," straining for adult approval, unable ever to be fully a child. The situation is similar in poetry, as poets of all ages, races, social classes, sexes, and sexual preferences twist themselves into psychic pretzels fighting for the rewards of Establishment approval. Fighting to be *mature*.

To demonstrate how much is lost by accepting the standard view of maturity, I've chosen two quite different poems from two extremely different poets. Suzanne Lummis is a leading exponent of the LA-based style known as Stand Up Poetry. Charles Bukowski, more than a decade after his death, is still the poetic embodiment of the rogue male. Neither Lummis's nor Bukowski's poem is mature by Establishment standards. But both poems are intelligent, freshly perceived, and memorable depictions of the human condition.

To the Man in the Parking Lot of Sunset and Western
by Suzanne Lummis

I was the redhead at the window
of a moving 22 bus.
I was trying to open the window
to wave, shout "I love you!"
or "How 'bout lunch?"
or "Save me!"
or "Name your price!"

You were there with your friend.
You had come to this place
on a motorcycle—not the rough-neck kind
with lots of metal and stupid parts.
Yours was designer-sleek, looked
like in good hands, it could fly, crash
the back gate of heaven.
You were the one in the black satin jacket
that fit, jeans that fit,
satin-black hair, shoulders,
Hollywood eyes, and who was worth cold cash
just from the waist up.

I was the one on my way
to get my car from the shop.
If I'd had my car I'd have parked it
and run to you acting hysterical.
I'd have said, "I'll make you a star!"
or, "I know my body's not enough.
I'll bring friends!"
And later, calmer,
over drinks I'd say, "Babe,
you're a high-stake game.
I'll play."

But the window was jammed. Everyone stared,
first at me then, following my eyes,

at you.
The bus took off with a burst
of dirt-colored smoke, and later
I bet some hussy got you, married you
for the good times and the bad news.

No good asking what's a heartstop like you
doing in the lot
of a laundromat, Fast Chicken and 7-11.
Why's a gem like me
being carried off in this horrible bus,
to a greasy and horrible garage,
and probably to some other horrible place after that
without you?

No good saying, "I love you."
It's late
and I'm on my own.
Who would hear?[136]

In this poem, Lummis takes a number of risks, and makes them pay off. She is openly, defiantly glib—and very funny—in the lines she wants to speak to the man.

She is flagrantly sexist. The man is purely a sex object. The speaker doesn't know anything about his mind and/or his soul, and doesn't care. She'd buy him for a night if she could; he's "worth cold cash just from the waist up."

She's also sexist in her treatment of women, including herself. When she says "I know my body's not enough," she assumes that women's worth to men is based solely on sex. She accepts the man's assumed conditions unconditionally, for herself and other women: she'll "bring friends." She even calls her hypothetical competition a "hussy"—hardly a term of sisterhood.

---

136 Suzanne Lummis, "To the Man in the Parking Lot at Sunset and Western" in *In Danger* (Berkeley: Heyday Books, 1999): 20.

Lummis's narrative is straightforward and clear. There is no "mysterious"[137] imagery. There is none of the falsely lyrical or fashionably "non-sequential" structure that Steve Kowit lampoons brilliantly in the *New York Quarterly*.[138] Lummis rejects more literary adjectives to label motorcycle parts "stupid" and several things "horrible"—the comically apt language of common speech. And in the end she takes the greatest literary risk of all: sentimentality. With no protective imagistic flourishes, absolutely no rhetorical shielding, the speaker admits that she is lonely and afraid.

In this poem, Lummis allows her speaker to be flippant, sexist, superficial, adolescent, obvious. Her poem is not somber or earnest. It is playful and enthusiastic, uses humor liberally, indulges in a flight of sophomoric romantic fancy, and is easy and fun to read and understand. It is steeped in popular culture, riddled with bad taste and politically incorrect attitudes. It is not world-weary; rather, it is weary of not getting *enough* of the world. It is hyperbolic, overstated, unrestrained.

It is also bright, witty, and carefully crafted. It uses language in a charged and unpredictable way. It is insightful, poignant, entertaining, honest—the poem of a strongly sexual woman not writing about how things are supposed to be, but how they are; not portraying herself as the Establishment wants women to be, but as, caught up in the emotion of the moment, she is.

In an earlier essay,[139] I contend that the best poems have historically been clear, and I distinguish four levels of clarity. A poem with *surface clarity* can be readily followed, and doesn't need translating or deciphering. A poem with *imagistic clarity* has sharp, apt, and memorable imagery. A poem with *dramatic clarity* has a strong sense of momentum and purpose; each line makes us eager to read the next. A poem with *psychological clarity* leads readers—generally by means of the other clarities—toward psychological/emotional insight. I believe that Lummis's poem achieves

---

137 "Mysterious [is] the poetry establishment's favorite tag for the imposing but impenetrable image." Kowit, "The Present State of American Poetry XII," 107.

138 "Start off with three or four perfectly clear descriptive lines, preferably soaked in middle-class angst . . . By line four or five, preferably in midsentence, one . . . slides into a sententious universal . . . At that point two or three lines that have nothing whatsoever to do with the original matter of the poem are absolutely mandatory. Preferably another fugitive memory, but looking, syntactically, as if it is inextricably connected to the lines that preceded it so that it's hard for the reader to know exactly where he's lost the thread. Bring in railroad tracks among the Queen Anne's lace right about here . . . and you've got it knocked." Ibid., 108–109.

139 Charles H. Webb, "In Defense of Clarity," first published in *The New York Quarterly* 46 (1992).

all four levels of clarity, and that its "immature" qualities contribute most to its psychological clarity, and thus to its success as a poem.

In his poem "trouble with spain,"[140] (text available on the Internet), Charles Bukowski also eschews the trappings of maturity to create a poem full of insight, wry humor, and visceral intensity.

The narrative is simple. Bukowski the poet, playing himself, is famous enough to be invited to an upscale literary party, but feels out of place and awkward, knowing he is there to be a conversation piece. Ugly and uncouth, a battered street-tom in a room full of pampered tabbies, he tries to preserve his dignity and assert his worth. When he meets a handsome cartoonist named Spain, Bukowski announces, "I like that name: Spain. / but I don't like you. why don't we step out / in the garden and I'll kick the shit out of your / ass."

Lucky for Spain, the hostess intervenes ". . . and rubbed his [Spain's] pecker / while I went to the crapper / and heaved." Bukowski's best efforts can't provoke a fight. He can't find the right posture, the right persona—not with Spain; not with anyone. He is expected to drink and leer and carry on; that is his role as gutter-poet. But he is also mocked and criticized for playing it—and simply for getting old. Even when he takes a shower after the party, nothing goes right. "I not only burnt my balls in that shower," he laments. "I spun around to get out of the burning / water, and burnt my bunghole / too." His manhood suffers either way.

The language of "trouble with spain" is unabashedly vulgar. The imagery is mainly sexual and/or excretory. Far from seeming urgent, essential, serious, this poem seems to have been tossed off as casually as Bukowski "went to the crapper and heaved." His language is so casual, in fact, that he doesn't bother to capitalize correctly, and succumbs to the dreaded comma-fault. He also indulges in macho posturing, drunken belligerence, bald-faced envy, self-justification, and self-pity. His attitude is not cool, not detached, not superior (although he tries briefly to pretend that *he* is). "trouble with spain" is, on the surface, callous and crude, the drunken grumbling of an old bum. Bukowski's noblest ambition seems to be escaping the shower without winding up in the burn ward.

The fact that this poem is hilarious is further evidence of immaturity—and not just Bukowski's. Any literate sixth grader could read this poem, and know exactly what is going on.

---

140 Charles Bukowski, *Burning in Water, Drowning in Flame, Selected Poems 1955-1973* (Santa Rosa: Black Sparrow Press, 1980).

"trouble with spain" will seem, to some, a good argument for preserving the concept of maturity, and using it to keep this kind of work as far away as possible from "real" poetry. The extent to which this has been accomplished, however, constitutes a loss for American poetry.

"trouble with spain" is, in fact, a powerful and comically tragic self-portrait. Bukowski does not give us the pretty posing of the dignified, mature poet; he gives us Man—naked, aging, prey to all vicissitudes of the flesh, and unable to find a place to stand comfortably in the world. This is the human condition, and the stuff of poetry.

I could list many more examples of the losses arising from the current concept of maturity. Wanda Coleman writes powerful and poignant poetry in a black idiom that makes the Establishment uncomfortable. Allen Ginsberg's gay poems, after all these years, still get the Establishment squirming. Gerald Locklin, as learned as any Establishment don, has published thousands of his often scurrilous, always entertaining poems, without winning one major national prize. Ron Koertge writes brilliantly in the voice of the young male:[141] horny, explicit, and side-splittingly funny. His book *High School Dirty Poems*[142] flies directly in the face of what passes for maturity, and could, if widely known, bring legions of new readers to poetry.[143]

Creative people of all ages see the world with "new eyes," as children do. They see the dunghill under the lily, and the lily about to burst from the dunghill. As in fairy tales, they see when the Emperor has no clothes, and when a naked beggar is or should be Emperor. They have not been programmed so thoroughly that their perceptions have been frozen for all time, or that their wonder and amusement at the universe has dimmed.

All of which is not to say that some poets aren't victims of arrested development. This may or may not be a problem, depending on the poet's intended audience and his/her ability. Such a poet may even achieve universality by speaking to the child in us all.

In his poem "Poop," Gerald Locklin—a patriarchal figure in his life off the page—achieves universality by letting a child—literally—speak to us all.

---

141 Educators decry the lack of male interest in reading—especially in reading literature, and most especially in reading poetry. One big reason is that their point of view is under- and/or fraudulently represented.

142 Ronald Koertge, *High School Dirty Poems* (Los Angeles: Red Wind Books, 1991).

143 Since this essay was first published, Koertge has won acclaim as a writer of Young Adult fiction.

Poop

> my daughter, blake, is in kindergarten. they are teaching her to be a
>   docile citizen and, incidentally to read. concurrently, like many of
>   us, she has become a trifle anal compulsive. complications ensue.
>
> i ask her what she has learned today. she says, "i learned the pledge
>   of allegiance." "how does it go?" i ask. "it goes," she says, "i poop
>   allegiance to the poop of the united poops of ameripoop."
>
> "that's good," i say, "that's very good. what else?" "o say can you
>   poop, by the dawn's early poop, what so proudly we pooped . . ."
>
> for christmas, she improvises, "away in a pooper, all covered with
>   poop, the little lord poopus lay pooping his poop."
>
> she has personalized other traditional favorites as well. someone,
>   perhaps her grandmother, tried to teach her the "our father." her
>   version goes, "our pooper, who art in poopland, hallowed be thy
>   poop. thy poopdom poop, thy poop be pooped, on earth as it is in
>   poopland."
>
> surely hemingway would feel one-upped. surely the second pooping
>   is at hand.
>
> a fortune teller told us blake would be our greatest sorrow and our
>   greatest joy. already, it is true.[144]

The impact of this, perhaps Locklin's best known poem, comes directly
from its childishness. Unable to understand the importance of adult symbols, kindergartener Blake heaps "poop" on God and country with unabashed delight. Is this ignorance, or innate wisdom that our society tries
to stamp out through Education? To Blake, for whom the world is a giant
toy chest full of new things to explore, her verbal improvisations celebrate
an amazing substance and a potent word. Compared to this, adult abstrac-
tions are not worth . . . you know.

---

144 Locklin, *Poop and Other Poems*, 12.

Locklin, the adult poet, sets his daughter's compositions in a larger context, thus producing a poem rich with adult ambiguities. The sacred cows of our culture are full of poop; they are also sacred. They are meaningless—and they fill a deep human need for meaning. Blake's observations delight the poet for any number of reasons, and make him sad for the same reasons. By communicating Blake's experience, as well as his experience of Blake and her experience, Locklin's poem embodies the very mysteries that religion and patriotism try to explain and control. The paradox of life's dualities—joy/sorrow, pleasure/pain, life/death—is presented with wit, compassion, and simplicity, making this poem, which I have heard denounced as crass and immature, ring deep and true.

If I could, I would banish *mature* from the critical lexicon. Since I can't, I'd like to venture some suggestions. When we see the word applied to poetry, let's be clear exactly what it means: poetry that seems fully developed and ripe *according to the moral and philosophical values of the person using the word*. Let's not try to force all poetry into the same Procrustean bed. Since it is human nature to discriminate—i.e., to judge—let's try to judge poetry on its own terms: children's poetry, adolescent poetry, young men's poetry, young women's poetry, working-class poetry, upper-class poetry, etc. Let's admit openly, even proudly, that our judgments are subjective; one person's maturity may be another's fuddy-duddy-dom.

I have no wish to overthrow mainstream or avant-garde/experimental poetry. As a white, middle-class college professor, I enjoy some of it myself. What I wish for is a broadening of the spectrum, an expanding of what is deemed acceptable, and a breaking down of hidden and unexamined biases that work against the vitality and relevance of American poetry.

Maturity is the varnish of socialization with which we try to hide the naked truth that we are all babies inside. Socialization is, by definition, useful in social interaction. It makes the world run more smoothly. But it exacts a price: estrangement from self, and from the source of the best art. When I open a book of poems, I don't want good breeding and accepted verities. I want liveliness, imagination, fervor, and when called for, ferocity. I want explorations of ever-changing, always-relative human truths, presented in engrossing, entertaining ways. Asked to choose between that and what passes for maturity, I'll take immaturity every time.

A Defense of Humor in Poetry

More than 2000 years after Aristotle declared Tragedy superior to Comedy, humor in poetry still gets, if not exactly no respect, not very much. Place a humorous book—however deft, imaginative, insightful, lyrical, and fundamentally serious—in a major competition with a just-plain-serious one, and the just-plain-serious will likely prevail. The sales and popular success of former Poet Laureate Billy Collins have been, by poetry's standard, phenomenal; yet he is "dissed," regularly and vehemently, in ways and amounts that less humorous ex-Laureates are not. Mainstream poetry has at least partially absorbed the influence of Stand Up Poetry[145]; but it does so, I think, apologetically: "So-and-So is funny, true. But he can really *write*."

Strange that humor in poetry requires a defense, while humor in serious novels, movies, and plays does not. Because poetry is not winnowed in the marketplace, the Romantic emphasis on simple, edifying emotion and guileless sincerity has lingered longer and stayed stronger in poetry than in the other literary arts—this despite the fact that, of English Romantic Poetry's "Big Three," Keats used humor often in his letters[146]; and Byron, in his poetry.

Pound, too, used humor in his work; Stevens was whimsical and playful. Even Eliot—not a man we picture with a lampshade on his head—created an iconic comic figure in Prufrock. Yet poetic Modernism comes across as deadly serious.

---

145 "Not every Stand Up poem is fall-down funny, but many make skillful use of humor. Playful, irreverent, and high-spirited, these poems employ the techniques of comedy: timing, absurdity, hyperbole." Webb, *Stand Up Poetry: An Expanded Anthology*, xviii.

146 In the "Age of Pope" that preceded the Romantics, poetical humor in English needed no defense.

Perhaps the growing estrangement of poetry from popular readership allowed the art to move away from what evolutionary psychologist Geoffrey Miller calls "natural human taste,"[147] and to develop a more elitist, less reader-friendly aesthetic. In any case, the humor-in-poetry situation is better than it was in the smug 1950s, though not nearly as good as it should be.

To use humor frequently, even to very serious ends, puts a poet's reputation at risk. I've heard James Tate—better known for wild, surreal humor than for his exception-proves-the-rule Pulitzer—called "not a poet at all." When I met Kenneth Koch, and thanked him for blazing a path for other humorous poets, he shot back, "I'm not a humorous poet," with all the heat of a pro boxer denying he is gay. A mutual friend told me later, "Kenneth thinks that being seen as funny has hurt his career."

Yet, just as a good sense of humor makes for better conversation, it also makes for better Art. Aristotle notwithstanding, Comedy is better suited than Tragedy to capture the absurdities, enormities, and pathos of twenty-first century life.

The "death of God" in the late nineteenth century dealt High Seriousness a mortal blow.[148] If an all-knowing, all-powerful Deity rules the world—if that Deity has a plan for the betterment and final salvation/damnation of humankind—it's not a laughing proposition. The God who tortured Job and sent His own son to be crucified was no comedian.

Evolution unwittingly is.[149] Chance is too, and its handmaiden, Probability.

If no wise God made humankind, ordaining us to dominate the earth, our high opinion of ourselves may be delusional; our desires and passions, less grand and noble than we like to think. Watch a troop of impassioned chimpanzees; then try to tell yourself that we aren't much the same. High Seriousness may well be high absurdity. And if one function of Art is to accurately portray the world, absurdity must be part of that portrayal.

Without God as Cosmic Umpire, morality becomes not a series of divine commandments, but a highly fallible, variable, and sometimes laughable set of rules devised by people for their own purposes. Even if evolu-

---

147 Geoffrey Miller, *The Mating Mind* (New York: Anchor Books, 2000): 284.

148 Although, like one of Kurosawa's samurai bisected by a master's blade, poetic High Seriousness seems oblivious to what has happened.

149 Consider the platypus, anteater, wildebeest . . .

tion has given us the template of a moral sense, it's a far cry from stone tablets inscribed by God's own hand.

If, then, even "well-born" people aren't inherently noble, and no Absolute Moral Truth exists, the Tragedy that Aristotle extolled starts to deflate. Doubt and Subjectivity move to the forefront of Philosophy; and Comedy, to the forefront of Art.

This is not a bad thing. Just as people love to eat, drink, and have sex, they love to laugh. Laughter is, as psychologists say, reinforcing. It gives pleasure. And traits that reinforce the brain with pleasure generally have survival value. Laughter would not have evolved and persisted in *Homo sapiens* if it carried no benefits.

1. Catharsis

Laughing feels a lot like weeping, even down to the tears. It also feels, in many ways, like orgasm. Breath is disrupted, the body convulsed in similar ways. Feelings of relief, tension-release, and relaxation occur. These may be psychologically good for the weeper. For the laugher and the lover, they *always* are.

2. Health benefits

There is much evidence that laughter helps people physiologically. Norman Cousins's self-healing via Marx Brothers movies is only the best-known of many examples.

3. Social bonding

The good spirits induced by laughter help to create a sense of friendship and community. People who laugh together are more likely to cooperate, and less likely to fight.

4. Enhanced personal effectiveness

Finding humor in a difficult situation offers a sense of power over and superiority to that situation, as when one pictures a dominating boss in funny underwear. The difficulty is made to seem more manageable. And it's well-known that people who believe they can be effective are more likely to be.

5. Aggression

The use of humor to ridicule rivals and/or enemies can raise the status of the humorist, lower the status of his/her target, and sometimes, take the place of physical violence.[150]

The effects of humor in poetry are just as strong.

1. Likeability

A good poem depends on voice. And people like a voice spiced with humor. Humorless poems may have other good qualities; but reading them, the bonding effect of laughter, by which people recognize shared understanding and pleasure, does not occur. Effective use of humor adds to the believability of an author's voice, and imbues it with humanity.

2. Evidence of intelligence

Like facility with metaphor, a good sense of humor requires mental quickness and the ability to make unusual connections. Since poetry, like all the arts, depends on a display of special skills, the intellectual adroitness of humor adds to a poem's general positive effect.

3. Originality

Humor is a good way to, as Ezra Pound enjoins poets, "Make it new." In many cases, the comic vein is less mined than more serious ones. Faced with writing a love lyric, a poem of political outrage, or even a lament or elegy, humor can add needed freshness.

4. Philosophy made engaging

Humor also allows the poet to deal effectively with philosophical issues—including postmodern ones—without resorting to audience-alienating "avant-garde" techniques. Slippery narrators, fragmentation of experience, lack of closure, unreliability of language, moral relativism, indeterminacy, the problem of *meaning*, etc., can be explored and interrogated while keeping readers engaged and entertained.

In keeping with our Puritan tradition, Art of any kind is suspect for many American adults. Suspicion may be allayed if the art is painful: sad, grim, and/or self-punishing; pious as a parson; sober as a Mormon judge; honest

---

150 Other times, of course, humor may provoke it.

as an abscess; "good for you" in the way bad-tasting potions were once thought to be.[151]

Among poets, the most damning adjective is not *pompous*, not *prim*, *prating*, *preening*, *self-righteous*, *obfuscating*, *obvious*, not even *tedious*, *boring*, or *dull*; it is *easy*, as if the cardinal sin of poetry is to relax and not work hard. High spirits, energy, and fun are kid stuff, according to this view—charming, perhaps, in a simple-minded way, but not the right stuff for real art, real Poetry.

Yet negative emotions—sorrow, anger, guilt, fear, regret—are no more "deep" and "true" than positive ones such as happiness, confidence, delight. Any two-year-old can whine and cry. Most twelve-year-olds can speak at length on *Why Life Sucks*. It takes more depth of character to grasp the inevitability of suffering, yet laugh anyway. Good humorous poems are far from *easy*. Those who doubt this should try writing one. Laughter is as hard-won and authentic an artistic response as tears—and may be more enlightening and healthful, too.

Some poets—Billy Collins, James Tate, Denise Duhamel, Russell Edson, David Kirby spring to mind—may be best known for humor. Others are not well-enough known for it. William Trowbridge and Roger Weingarten have been writing seriously funny poems for years. Gerald Locklin is best known as an "underground" poet. Suzanne Lummis is best known in LA; Steve Kowit, in San Diego. Ron Koertge has turned his hand to Young Adult novels, where his talent for humor has won acclaim.

Other poets, including Stephen Dobyns, Amy Gerstler, Tony Hoagland, Bob Hicok, Barbara Hamby, and Lynn Emanuel, though not identified so strongly, perhaps, as "funny" poets, use a lot of humor in their work.

Catherine Bowman, in "No Sorry,"[152] uses hyperbole to make serious political and moral points. The poem begins with person A asking person B to borrow a pair of scissors. The requests escalate until A is asking B, "Do you have any thermonuclear warheads? . . . Got any enhanced tactical neutron lasers emitting massive doses of whole-body gamma radiation? . . . Got any chemical agents, nerve agents, blister agents . . . any choking agents or incapacitating agents or toxin agents?" By the time the poem ends with the image of a butter knife passed down to A by her grandfather, it's hard not to feel that the human love of weaponry is both ridiculous and horrible, and should be abandoned right away.

---

151 If humor does appear, the learned kind is preferred, being the product of arduous years.
152 Catherine Bowman, "No Sorry," in *Stand Up Poetry: An Expanded Anthology*, 23.

Richard Garcia's "Chickens Everywhere"[153] opens on a comic world where chickens sing Glenn Miller's "In the Mood," a beautiful woman parts her bathrobe to reveal a chicken peeking from between her legs, and our own pet chicken (naturally we have one) grows six feet tall. Then the mood, which has been comically surreal, turns tender, beautiful, and frightening. "Walk alone in the night. Keep your collar up and your head down. The night is a chicken with enormous black wings. And you, little one, are a grain of wheat on the floor of a barn."

The speaker in Kim Addonizio's "For Desire,"[154] could easily seem histrionic and self-obsessed with her demands for "the strongest cheese," "the good wine," her lover at her feet praising her beauty. But the speaker's excesses are mitigated by humor. No one can speak of kisses that ". . . arrive by the boatload, / and begin their delicious diaspora / through the cities and small towns of my body," yet be unaware of the comic aspects of desire and narcissistic need. ". . . I want to / lie down somewhere and suffer for love until / it nearly kills me . . ." both embraces and pokes fun at the countless movies, books, and songs about people who, with no such self-awareness, destroy themselves for love. And when the speaker wishes for her lover to "come over here and get down on your knees and tell me just how fucking good I look," the comically colloquial use of *fucking*, coupled with the stark honesty of her fantasy—who wouldn't wish it? how many of us have the courage to admit it?—wins this reader over all the way. Addonizio has her cake and gobbles it, writing a poem that makes fun of passion, while indulging in it shamelessly.

In the following poem, Mark Halliday uses humor to address, among other things, humankind's post-existential, postmodern predicament.

Trumpet Player, 1963

> *And when I get to Surf City, I'll be shootin' the curls,*
> *And checkin' out the parties for surfer girls.*

When Jan and Dean recorded "Surf City"
there must have been one guy—
I see this trumpet player (was there even a horn section in that song?
Say there was)—

---

153 Richard Garcia, "Chickens Everywhere," in *Stand Up Poetry: An Expanded Anthology*, 110.
154 Kim Addonizio, "For Desire," in *Stand Up Poetry: An Expanded Anthology*, 1.

I see this one trumpet player with his tie askew
or maybe he's wearing a loose tropical-foliage shirt
sitting on a metal chair waiting
for the session to reach the big chorus
where Jan and Dean exult
"Two girls for every boy"
                              and he's thinking
of his hundred nights on his buddy Marvin's hairy stainy sofa
and the way hot dogs and coffee make a mud misery
and the way one girl is far too much and besides
he hasn't had the one in fourteen months, wait,
it's fifteen now.
Surfing—what life actually lets guys ride boards
on waves? Is it all fiction? Is it a joke?
Jan and Dean and their pal Brian act like it's a fine good joke
whereas this trumpet player thinks it's actually shit,
if anybody asked him, a tidal wave of shit.
Nobody's asking.
The producer jiggles in his headphones. He wants more drums
right after *all you gotta do is just wink your eye!*
This producer is chubby and there is no chance,
my trumpet player thinks, that this chubhead gets
two swingin' honeys at any party ever and besides
on a given night a man only has one cock, or
am I wrong? And besides, you wake up wanting five aspirin
in an air lousy with lies, or half-lies.
And that's with only one girl.
But why am I so pissed here, he thinks,
when all these guys are hot for a hit?
Because I'm deep like Coltrane and they're all shallow,
right? Or because
I'm this smelly sour session man with a bent nose,
and they're all hip to this fine fine joke?

The song is cooking, it's nearly in the can,
everybody has that hot-hit look
and my trumpet man has a thought: Sex

is not really it—what they're singing about—
they're singing about being here.
This dumb song is *it*:
this studio, this is the only Surf City,
here. And that's the great joke.

Okay, surf dicks, I am hip. But
there's gonna be pain in Kansas, he thinks,
lifting his horn and watching for the cue,
when they hear about Surf City and believe it.[155]

This is a poem of voice—two voices actually, which overlap and blend. One voice belongs to "I," the narrator who creates the trumpet player and tells his story; the other, to the trumpet player: a character so fictional that the narrator is not even sure there was a trumpet on "Surf City." Most of the poem's humor comes from the voices of the narrator and the trumpet player, which sound (not coincidentally) the same: cynical, colloquial, profane.

"Trumpet Player, 1963" is no sweet-sounding lyric or bardic prophesy. The phrase "hairy, stainy sofa" is funny and descriptive, but purposely talky and awkward, the two *y*'s a far cry from mellifluous. "Mud misery" alliterates in a catchy way, but the phrase is more comic than poignant or beautiful. "Trumpet Player, 1963" is what Nicanor Parra called "antipoetry," using everyday language to describe everyday life.

A tone of cynicism and mockery is established with the epigraph from "Surf City," by the perpetually off-key Jan and Dean. The narrator lets us know by lines three and four that he is less concerned with facts than with a funny line—and the creative act. Was there a horn section? he asks; then answers, with the God-like power of the artist, "Say there was."

The trumpet player is announced as fictional; yet the power of voice makes him seem real, "tie askew," wearing a "tropical foliage shirt" that parodies the beach paradise his music celebrates. We don't know how good a trumpet player he is, but he's presumably better than his small part in "Surf City." He's certainly too smart for his own good, using the inflated verb "exult" to spoof the "big chorus," *Two girls for every boy*. Both the trumpet player and the narrator know well that "Ode to Joy" is a "big chorus" that "exults"; "Surf City" is a tiny piece of schlock.

---

155 Mark Halliday, *Jab* (Chicago: University of Chicago Press, 2002).

Still, for the males in Jan and Dean's audience, *Two girls for every boy* defines heaven *and* joy. Our trumpeter knows better. In real life—as if he were real—one girl is "far too much." When, later, he describes "waking up wanting five aspirin / in an air lousy with lies, or half-lies" the trumpeter is at his jaded, heartbroken, defeated, and bitterly comic best. He hasn't had a girl in fourteen months—"wait, it's fifteen now"; but who's counting? He can feign nonchalance all day; the truth still hurts.

Now he confronts the central question of the poem. Is the surfing life "all fiction? Is it a joke?"

How many cherished beliefs—that love conquers all, that truth will out, that cheaters never prosper, that good people go to heaven—may be cruel jokes? A man scrimps all his life, saving for retirement, then dies in its first month. A woman trusts the justice system, and ends up a quadruple victim as her rapist walks, his lawyer abuses her, and her lawyer cashes in. You join the army to fight for your country, go on a mission designed to make some General look good, and come home with two stumps and a hook.

A few people—Jan, Dean, Brian Wilson, the "chubby" producer— seem to love the surfing life. But to the trumpet player, it's "a tidal wave of shit." Beyond his pay for this session, he gets no rewards: artistic, monetary, or otherwise. He doesn't surf. He's not a singer or even a guitar player, just the backup of the backup. He may not even exist; that's how much of a joke he is. No wonder "Nobody's asking" what he thinks.

The producer, a philistine who calls in extra drums to pump up the cosmic drama of "All you've gotta do is just wink your eye," is, to the trumpeter, a total joke: a "chubhead" who has "no chance" of getting "two swinging honeys," any time or anywhere. The trumpeter states this as Fact; yet he must know, deep down, that if the producer scores a hit with "Surf City," chubby or not, he can have all the swinging honeys he wants.

Now the trumpeter—and narrator—stop to reflect, "Why am I so pissed here ... ?"

The words are the trumpeter's, but with "he thinks" coming *after* the phrase, the question could come from the narrator too. The trumpeter (narrator?) wants to believe he's the archetypal Great Artist, doomed to suffer while lesser talents thrive. That belief may have consoled him in the past; but it fails now. He knows he's no Coltrane, just "a smelly, sour session man with a bent nose," excluded from the "fine fine joke" going on around him.

Then, epiphany: Jan and Dean and the other "surf dicks" are not celebrating surf, or sex, or endless youthful possibility; they're singing about
the joy of making myths—getting rich duping the rest of the world. Surf
City—i.e., heaven—is making hits. It's being in the money, in the action,
in the know. It's creating—however debased the final product—Art.

That's not the whole story, though. The phrase "my trumpet man has
a thought" reminds us again that the horn-guy is the narrator's creation:
doubly untrustworthy when he insists that Jan and Dean's listeners will
be hurt to learn Surf City isn't "real." If a fiction is maintained for long
enough, it can become indistinguishable from truth. This is the biggest
joke of all. For every Kansas boy who trekked to LA and found Surf City
a lie, thousands stayed home, and may have died as True Believers—died,
and lived more happily for their belief.

"Trumpet Player, 1963" is not "Fern Hill." It won't, most likely, bring a
lump to the throat or tears to the eyes; but neither do most non-humorous
poems. What this poem brings is serious comic entertainment. It gives
readers a colorful and fascinating character to enjoy, plus a fuller understanding of art (and Art), the slipperiness of "I," the sadness of the outsider,
and the difficulty of separating *fictional* from *true*.

That, it seems to me, is quite a lot.

One big question remains:[156] If humor adds so much to poetry, why
doesn't the whole literary world—especially poets—acknowledge the fact,
and honor skilled practitioners? In 2004, *Poetry* magazine presented its
first Mark Twain Poetry Award for Humor; but Mark Twain is known
as a novelist and essayist, not as a poet. There is no Hart Crane prize for
humor in poetry. No Elizabeth Bishop prize, or Derek Walcott Prize, or
Seamus Heaney prize. If there were an Ogden Nash prize, it would be for
light verse.

Are readers of poetry more likely than other readers to cherish a sense
of propriety that humor offends? My own experience says this is true.
Long viewed as the pinnacle of verbal art, poetry attracts more than its
share of readers who see their own taste as some kind of pinnacle. Such
readers not infrequently maintain an elevated sense of their own intelligence, sensitivity, dignity, and importance, all of which can lead to hy-
per-seriousness, or even what psychologists call—I'm not making this up—
humor incompetence.

---

156 After, of course, you throw out "Of what does dark matter consist?," "Is it wise to have sex
on the first date?," and a few more.

In addition, readers of poetry, like poets themselves, often have depressive temperaments. Nancy Andreasen's classic study of MFA students at the University of Iowa revealed a high incidence of psychopathology, with depression in the lead.[157] An article in the *British Journal of Psychiatry* found psychosis or depression in 80% of sampled poets.[158] James Kaufman's "The Sylvia Plath effect" contained similar findings, especially for female poets.[159] Since depressed people tend to see more sadness than humor in the world, it's not surprising that, even when they recognize it, they don't resonate with humor in poetry, and don't produce humorous poems themselves.[160] Conversely, people with a comedic turn of mind aren't likely to make their first literary stop at poetry.

But if poetry is, as it's been billed, the highest verbal expression of humankind—if it is, as Coleridge said, language used to optimal effect: "the best words in the best order"—poets are well-advised to use every resource their language provides. Why run on seven cylinders when your car has eight? Why use just fastballs if you can throw a good curve? For Billy Collins to change from a self-described writer of "bad imitations" into one of the more original voices in U.S. poetry, he had "to allow into my poetry aspects of my self—my sensibility and my experience—that I had been unwittingly censoring."[161] That meant, in Collins's case, his sense of humor.

I've emphasized the use of humor for serious purposes. But poems meant mainly for laughs can be good, too. James Tate's "Goodtime Jesus,"[162] which ends with Christ saying, "I love that donkey. Hell, I love everyone," primarily just cracks me up. Yet it does raise serious issues about Christianity, and religion in general. If the world is absurd, *funny* may also be *true*.

Clearly, humor is not required for a poem to be great. No poet should feel compelled to be funny, any more than to write beautiful lyrics about birds. The best humor, like Shakespeare's "quality of mercy," is not

---

157 Nancy Andreasen, "Creativity and mental illness: prevalence rates in writers and their first-degree relatives," *American Journal of Psychiatry* Vol. 144, Issue 10 (1987): 1288–92.

158 F. Post, "Verbal creativity, depression and alcoholism. An investigation of one hundred American and British writers," *British Journal of Psychiatry* 168, no. 5 (1996): 545–55.

159 J. C. Kaufman "The Sylvia Plath effect: Mental illness in eminent creative writers," *The Journal of Creative Behavior* 35, no. 1 (2001).

160 Bipolar poets may be very funny in the manic state.

161 Collins, "The End of Boredom," 155.

162 James Tate, *Selected Poems* (Hanover: Wesleyan University Press, 1991): 177.

strained; it rises naturally from the humorist's view of the world. Better no humor at all than the forced kind.

Still, just as it helps a poet to develop greater attention to details, or more facility with metaphor, it helps to cultivate a sense of humor. If humor is, or could be, part of a poet's personality, why not let it into the poems? They'll be more entertaining for it. And, very likely, deeper and more serious too.

How I Met the Prose Poem, and What Ensued

It was the '70s. In flared pants and angel-wing collar, I was browsing the University of Washington Bookstore, wishing that I had a book in there. One of two things happened next. Either I pulled Russell Edson's *The Intuitive Journey* out of the Poetry section, or a pteranodon dragging a sign—WILL GRONK FOR FOOD—swooshed overhead, and dropped the book into my hands.

This wasn't The Virgin Meets Gabriel; still, it was a revelation. I'd been writing lined poems for several years. I'd even published a few. But I was baffled by the odd poem-stories I sometimes scribbled to amuse myself. These stories used "poetic" metaphor and imagery; but they didn't fit comfortably into poetic lines, and were too short to be short stories. They also tended to be funny (to me, at least), and strange. One featured an animal with the face of a proboscis monkey and the body of a sea cucumber. Another concerned an air mattress that yearned to be a set of pan-pipes.

Writing these poem-stories was fun; but like cave-painting, there seemed to be no future in it. Now I saw that I'd been trying to invent the prose poem. Edson's book saved me the trouble. It also gave me models of excellence in the form, and from the credits, a list of magazines that might consider my attempts.

My next discovery—delivered by a man made entirely of Swedish meatballs, if memory serves—was Michael Benedikt's *Night Cries*. Seattle's nature poets and Roethke-worshippers had tended to find my work amusing, but not serious enough for Capital *P* Poetry. For my part, I found much poetry of that time to be pompous, sappy, self-righteous, and hyper-serious. Many poets not only wore their sensitivity on their sleeves, they tattooed it on their foreheads and combed their hair back so everyone would see.

Imagine my delight to find a section of *Night Cries* called "Insensitive Poems."

Prose poems allowed me to indulge—and exploit—parts of my psyche that had felt off-limits to "regular" poems. It was as if several cylinders that normally froze when I sat down to write, had broken free. My writing gained in horsepower, if not respectability. Prose poems exploded the self-importance that I had found (and still find) laughable in poetry. I enjoy good line breaks as much as the next guy, but to call a line break "daring," "thrilling," or even "exciting" seems on a par with calling a well-made business card "orgasmic."

The possibilities that the prose-poem opened for me *were* exciting. And continue to be. Prose poems give me unlimited license to be imaginative, outrageous, surreal, obscene, politically incorrect, satirical, silly, seditious, scathing, and even sensitive, while being at the same time (I hope) smart, insightful, and emotionally true. Prose poems allow me to float lightly over sentimental reefs that would sink more formal poems.

Prose poems today range from little poem-stories to postmodern clumps of unlined, non-sequential sentences. L=A=N=G=U=A=G=E poets write L=A=N=G=U=A=G=E prose poems. Prose poems can be pure lyrics or solemn meditations. Yet prose poems lend themselves especially well to wit and humor. The form itself is humorous: an oxymoron; the duck-billed platypus of poetry. And humor is a device ideally suited to depict the absurdities, enormities, and pathos of contemporary life. Eliot said that to capture the complexities of modern times, poetry had to be difficult. I say it has to be, at least sometimes, funny.

Writing prose poems has lowered my inhibitions when writing lined poems. The result is that I write fewer prose poems. Subject matter and attitudes that once would have screamed "Prose Poem!" are, today, as likely to give rise to lines. I often try my poems in both lines and prose, moving back and forth until I find what the poem seems to need. Even if not orgasmic, good line breaks can add to the impact of a poem. If they add to mine, I use them.

Still, a prose poem can be paced effectively with punctuation. Sound, rhythm, and internal rhyme can be mobilized as easily as in lined verse. And there is a casualness to prose poetry that recommends itself to me as writer, and to readers—even the poetry-phobes. If a poem of mine is narrative, wildly imaginative, uses dialogue, and—above all—seems to read more naturally and easily in prose, into prose it goes.

To write even the most informal lined poem always feels to me a bit like dressing up. That's great. I like nice pants and shirts, well-fitting jackets, well-made shoes—even the occasional tux. But I still love to slip on a tee-shirt, old sneakers, broken-in blue jeans, and to invite something strange—a computer named Bladdo, a self-dismembering guitarist, a woolly mammoth caught on a dry fly—to come and do what I think prose poems do best, which is (like any good musician) to play.

The Poem as Fitness Display

Americans love a certain kind of show-off: Babe Ruth, Muhammad Ali, Britney Spears. Asked, though, why we read or write poetry, few would include "to show off" on our lists. Yet, like a mockingbird blasting songs from a power line, a good poem is an impressive display.[163] "I'm superior to other men; you should go to bed with me," the skilled Elizabethan sonneteer told the ladies of his day.

Poems that lack meter and rhyme are less obvious *tours de force*. "Anyone can write like that," the layperson may say. Still, roughly the same abilities are employed in good free verse as in the formal kind—employed, and put on display. In the terms of evolutionary psychology, writers of good poems show *evolutionary fitness*. Good readers of poetry, as it turns out, do too.

Evolutionary Psychology and Poetry

Traits that display genetic excellence can be called *fitness indicators*. These may be direct (fleetness of foot, useful for chasing game and running from danger) or indirect (facial symmetry, which indicates good health and generally good genes). In either case, fitness indicators are observable reports from the hidden genetic world. By evolving to favor fitness indicators, members of a species favor mates most likely to produce viable offspring.

To draw well, a person must have excellent fine motor skills; to sing well, good lungs and a strong heart. To write well requires first-rate mental abilities.

In *The Mating Mind*, evolutionary psychologist Geoffrey Miller writes, "We find attractive those things that could have been produced only by

---

163 "Meter, rhythm, and rhyme make communication harder . . . These constraints make poetry more impressive than prose as a display of verbal intelligence and creativity." Miller, *The Mating Mind*, 379.

people with attractive, high-fitness qualities such as . . . energy . . . intelligence, creativity . . . the ability to learn difficult skills . . ."[164] Maybe artistic ability evolved directly: people favored mates who could draw, sing, dance, tell stories, compose poetry. Or maybe artistic abilities were indirect effects of survival-enhancing traits that were already being selected for. In any case, as the human brain developed, people came to view the products of artistic ability as *beautiful*, and the abilities themselves as admirable, enjoyable, worthy, and morally good.

Since many of the traits necessary to make art are also necessary to evaluate it, and since artistic ability can't be a useful fitness indicator unless it *can* be evaluated, the abilities to make art and to appreciate it evolved hand-in-hand.

How Difficult Should Poetry Be?

T. S. Eliot famously declared that "poets, in our civilization . . . must be *difficult*."[165] But *how* difficult?

"The fundamental challenge facing artists is to demonstrate their fitness by making something that lower-fitness competitors could not make,"[166] Geoffrey Miller states. T. S. Eliot, in "The Love Song of J. Alfred Prufrock," accomplishes this. Yet a poem must not only be difficult to make; it must be recognized as such, *and* judged successful. Any honest attempt to bench press 300 pounds is difficult; but the attempt can indicate fitness only if people realize how hard the lift is, and that it succeeds. A poem must not be so difficult to apprehend that the reader gives up, and/ or judges the poem a failed lift.

Hard-to-make need not mean hard-to-evaluate. I don't need a PhD to judge "David" beautiful. Nor do I need more training than the time I tried to sculpt a man in clay—and produced something like a bipedal nematode—to judge Michelangelo exceptionally skilled. Faced with "Prufrock," readers may have a harder time.

To apprehend a poem requires more cognitive effort and ability than to apprehend a statue, simply because words are more abstract. In addition, since a poet can't create whole objects as a sculptor can, but must evoke the whole with a few details, poetry requires an artful withholding of in-

---

164 Miller, *The Mating Mind*, 281.
165 T. S. Eliot, "The Metaphysical Poets," in *Selected Essays, 1917–1932* (New York: Harcourt, Brace, 1932).
166 Miller, *The Mating Mind*, 282.

formation, and leaves readers to fill in the gaps. The ability to understand good poetry constitutes, in fact, a fitness indicator *for the reader*, showing that he/she can perform the required mental feats, as well as keep up with the poet's (presumably first-rate) mind.

Such displays of mental fitness increase the reader's sense of status, self-esteem, and overall desirability. Good readers of poetry feel good about their ability. In the terms of behavioral psychology, their reading is reinforced, making it more likely to recur.

This is not the case if a poem is too easy or too hard to apprehend. The most successful poetry achieves a balance of difficulty, allowing both writer and reader to display high-fitness abilities.

"What do you get when you cross a mafioso with a L=A=N=G= U=A=G=E poet?"

"An offer you can't understand."

To make a good joke is hard. Timing is vital; compression, too. Some information—especially connections that can be inferred—must be withheld. The exact right information must be delivered in the exact right order, at the exact right time, in the exact right *amount* of time. Too few words, the listener loses the point. Too many words slows the joke, and lessens its impact.

"What do you get when you cross somebody in the mafia with somebody who writes L=A=N=G=U=A=G=E poems?" bruises the joke. "An offer it's difficult to understand," critically wounds it. "A proposal it's difficult to figure out" sends it to the morgue.

To "get" this joke requires something from the audience. They have to know what *mafioso* and *L=A=N=G=U=A=G=E poetry* mean. They also have to know that L=A=N=G=U=A=G=E poetry is notoriously hard to understand. They must have heard the phrase "an offer you can't refuse," and know that it's spoken by a mafioso.

They may remember that Marlon Brando, who played the mafioso, spoke with cotton (literally) in his mouth, and so was hard to understand. This adds to the joke, as it does to know that his phrase means, "An offer you *don't dare* refuse." No one can possibly get the joke, though, who doesn't see how a person who says "an offer you can't refuse," plus a person who writes poetry you can't understand, equals "an offer you can't understand."

A listener who sees the punch line coming will not laugh or experience much enjoyment, and may feel contemptuous. A listener who gets the joke too late loses enjoyment and satisfaction. A listener who doesn't get it at all not only won't enjoy it, but will judge either the joke or his/her intellect as lacking. Pleasure is not an option here.

For ideal impact, listeners must get the joke at the instant the punch line is pronounced, but must have done enough previous mental work—supplying withheld information and making connections—that a sense of their own intelligence and competence arrives in tandem with a sense of the joke's. For most listeners, the perfect joke is, therefore, *moderately* difficult to apprehend, and improves on scrutiny.

The situation is the same with poetry. If a poem is too easy to understand—if it seems that an average or less-than-average mind conceived the lines and/or aimed them at an average or less-than-average audience—the poet has not displayed exceptional fitness. Nor can readers display fitness by understanding the poem. Instead of enjoyment, readers feel disdain.

If the poem is too difficult to understand, readers can't judge the poet's fitness, and may lose self-esteem in the process. They feel stupid, dense, insensitive, out of the cultural loop—anything but intellectually fit. Even when readers know the writer is at fault, they feel frustrated and annoyed.

The literal meaning of these lines from W. S. Merwin's poem "How We Are Spared"[167] is clear. "At midsummer before dawn an orange light returns to the mountains / Like a great weight and the small birds cry out / And bear it up." Still, the poem requires some thought. To "get" the poem, the reader must understand that it is not literally true; it is mythic: an imaginative, pre-scientific explanation of a physical phenomenon. The reader must imagine orange light as very heavy. He/she must picture small birds lifting the heavy light—maybe in their beaks, or by getting their bodies under it—then must imagine the birds, not *singing* because it's dawn, and birds naturally sing at dawn, but "crying out" because the light is heavy as they lift it from behind the mountains to bring the world what humans call "dawn."

To understand the title, the reader must imagine a world without light, then understand how the birds, in their strength and bravery, spare us from eternal night.

Changing the poem to "At midsummer before dawn an orange light returns to the mountains / The small birds *seem to* cry out *as they seem to* bear *the light* up / Like a great weight" offers too much information,

---

167 W. S. Merwin, *Selected Poems* (New York: Atheneum, 1988).

making the poem too easy to understand. It also wrecks the rhythm, and generally diminishes the poetry.

"At midsummer before dawn, small birds sing / as orange light rises above the mountains" is literally true, and easier to understand than Merwin's poem, since it requires nothing from the reader beyond an understanding of basic English. If the words still qualify as poetry, though, it's of a lesser kind.

Like any good poem, "How We Are Spared" gains resonance on rereading. I relish the poem's vivid imagery: mountains in orange light, small birds crying out. I admire the simile *like a great weight.* I understand why the poem sounds so good: the rhymes and near-rhymes of *light, great, weight,* and *out,* with the extra "t" alliteration in *returns*; the assonance of *dawn* and *orange, light* and *cry.* These subtleties, and many more, undoubtedly influenced my first reading of the poem. Rereadings increase my consciousness of them, adding to my understanding and enjoyment, and my admiration of Merwin's ability.

The success of "How We Are Spared" depends on its reader being aware that few people could write such a good poem, *and* on the poem's being not obscure, not recondite, but moderately difficult to apprehend. The poem's impact is immediate, but the reader has had mental work to do, and is rewarded with aesthetic pleasure, as well as the sense of a job well done. Subsequent readings add to the poem's impact and the reader's self-esteem. Therefore, the reader admires and enjoys the poem.

Legitimate Displays, and Otherwise
Poetry populists clamor for poems to be *accessible.* I'd like that too. But no matter how clear and direct the poet tries to be, a good poem—compared to prose—presents some difficulties.

1. Compression
To arrange "the best words in the best order," the poet must achieve flawless timing and optimal compression, each word adding an essential piece to the poem taking shape within the reader's mind, while withholding enough that the reader has invigorating fill-in work to do. Words will likely work on several levels. Linguistic innovations may occur. Syntax and grammar may be stretched. In addition, readers must grasp and respond to figurative language.

The reader of a poem must, in other words, read in full possession of all faculties. The necessity for this is part of what makes a poem good, and counts as legitimate display.

2. The author's intelligence can create difficulty, too

Just as the rightness of Einstein's theories justified their difficulty, "The Waste Land" justifies its difficulty by rewarding readers who do the necessary work. Eliot's intellect offers a legitimate and impressive display for readers up to the challenge. It's worth noting, though, that Shakespeare managed to please *both* groundlings and the most sophisticated human minds.

3. The author's emotional IQ

Freud believed that great writers are the best psychologists. To resonate with a good poem requires emotional depth and understanding. This creates legitimate difficulty for the reader—and a worthy display-arena, too.

Good poems need not, however, be equally accessible to readers at all stages of life. There are poems for youth, poems for the middle-aged, poems for old age, as well as poems that span the generations. It is hard to appreciate a poem that deals with emotions and/or life-stages the reader has not experienced. This difficulty is limiting, but legitimate.

4. Arcane references

As fewer cultural reference points are widely shared, it becomes harder for authors to gauge their own accessibility—i.e., how much information they can reasonably withhold. Is it legitimate for a poet to assume a college graduate's level of cultural awareness? How about to sprinkle one's cantos with Greek, Latin, Provencal, Chinese characters, and other assorted esoterica? Pedantry for its own sake may indicate personal insecurity, lack of insight into others, or even mental illness, all of which suggest low fitness.

5. Difficulty Above and Beyond . . .

Because some modern poems are difficult works of genius, some poets write difficult poems in hopes that they'll be works of genius too. But the poem that withholds too much in order to protect the poet's ego and/or to appear impressive and "deep," is not just difficult; it's as poorly made as (and may be synonymous with) the poem with garbled syntax, inept pacing, wavering tone, botched imagery. Such poems may fool some readers some of the time, but are fundamentally illegitimate.

6. Strategies of reader-frustration

"Experimental" poems may intentionally thwart reader expectations for such qualities as closure, emotional engagement, and identifiable meaning. The theory behind such strategies—often highly political—gives rise to poems that are self-consciously, proudly, and impenetrably difficult. Poems arising from these strategies use extreme withholding—discontinuity, opacity, indeterminate syntax and diction, and whatever else they can— to confound and shift reader-expectations. The legitimacy of this kind of difficult poem requires further discussion.

How Does Extremely Difficult-to-Apprehend Poetry Survive and Thrive?

If the most aesthetically pleasing poetry requires high fitness to write, and is moderately difficult to apprehend, how can we explain the success—as measured by books published, grants received, prizes won, academic jobs secured—of poetry that is extremely hard to understand, yet does not necessarily require high fitness to write? How do we account for the professional success of poets who actively strive for obliquity, opacity, indeterminacy, and in some cases, boring monotony, and whose own work bears out their assumption that meaning does not exist?

"Folk aesthetics concerns what ordinary people find beautiful," Geoffrey Miller states. ". . . elite aesthetics concerns the objects of art that highly educated, rich elites learn are considered worthy of comment by their peers."[168]

"With folk aesthetics, the focus is on the art-object as a display of the creator's craft. With elite aesthetics, the focus is on the viewer's response as a social display,"[169] Miller states. ". . . Elites . . . often try to distinguish themselves from the common run of humanity by replacing *natural human tastes* [italics mine] with artfully contrived preferences . . . [by which they] can display their intelligence, learning ability, and sensitivity to emerging cultural norms."[170]

---

168 Miller, *The Mating Mind*, 284.
169 Ibid.
170 Ibid.

The ability to employ this social strategy may be a fitness indicator in its own right.[171] The fitness indicated, however, does not arise from poetry per se. Rather, the strategy steers poets and readers away from *natural human tastes*: the kind of poems that evolution prepared the human mind to admire and enjoy.[172] The preference for extremely difficult poetry may enhance the status and self-esteem of the elite; but like bound feet, elite aesthetics encourage poems to develop in grotesque ways, leading to the literary equivalent of a whole court hobbling because the queen is lame.

This is not to say that all innovative and/or difficult-to-apprehend poems are illegitimate. There's no doubt, too, that some people would prefer extremely difficult poems even if no status advantage were obtained. Yet the difficulty of telling bad-difficult from good-difficult advances the strategy of the elite, inadvertent and unconscious though that strategy may be.

"Most people want to be able to interpret works of art as indicators of the artist's skill and creativity," Miller states. "Certain styles of art make this difficult to do."[173] Most readers must either reject these styles, or rely on the judgment of critics and professors: the elite.

Like priests anointed sole interpreters of the gods, many critics and professors love difficult poetry. Difficult poems require more filling in of gaps, and therefore, more commentary than less difficult ones—more creativity, ingenuity, and fun for the commentators, and more chances to shine, advance professionally, and display fitness. Since poetic reputations are born and maintained in universities, difficult poets tend to rise in the academic air, driving out the easier-to-understand.

Many poets, too, prefer their own poems to be very difficult. Difficulty erects a screen between writer and audience, protecting the writer from self-revelation, and deflecting criticism. Incomprehensibility may confer invulnerability. Furthermore, writing difficult poems may reassure writers who doubt their own talent and/or intelligence. As we have seen, difficult poems may pass for poems of genius.

---

171 I watched a student writer transform himself from a plain-spoken neo-Bukowski to a cryptologist-in-verse, blatantly seeking to carve a niche for himself in my class, and to increase his cachet with female students. His strategy worked, too!

172 For a defense of the concept of natural human taste, see Joseph Carrol, *Evolution and Literary Theory* (Columbia: University of Missouri Press, 1994), and Steven Pinker, *The Blank Slate: The Modern Denial of Human Nature* (New York: Viking, 2002).

173 Miller, *The Mating Mind*, 285.

By writing difficult poems, and admiring the difficult poems of others, poets elevate themselves to a Parnassus from which they can look down on the mob, bemoaning America's cultural collapse, and explaining their shrunken audience as a case of pearls before swine.

Since many poets are professors, they may prefer difficult poems for professorial reasons, too. For some "poetry professionals," difficult poetry may be a means to rise in the world. Working their careers like ambitious business-people, poetry professionals pursue success—academic advancement, readings, publications, prizes, salary—through networking, favor-trading, intimidation, and all other possible means, including writing and championing very difficult poems.

Self-delusion also enters the mix. Most difficult bad poets think they're good poets. They may even think they are accessible.

When it comes to writing very difficult poems, no group surpasses the L=A=N=G=U=A=G=E poets.[174] Their philosophy of poetry not only encourages difficulty, but demands it. In their distrust of meaning—especially the author-directed kind—L=A=N=G=U=A=G=E poets may withhold virtually all overt connections, seeking to shift responsibility from poet to reader. This makes for enormous difficulties when the reader is expected, in effect, to create a good poem from what may seem less-than-nothing.

To the long list of reasons for the flourishing of very difficult poetry, add the fact that many readers—overmatched, or casualties of bad teaching—can't tell the difference between difficult good and difficult bad poems. Here, the Emperor's New Clothes Syndrome comes into play: Poet A wins the Formidable Prize. Reader Z can't understand A's poems and, on a gut level, doesn't like them. However, Z recognizes and applauds the many competing aesthetics in American poetry, and does not wish to appear narrow-minded, intolerant, judgmental, or dense. And what is Z's judgment worth, compared to that of the Judges who chose A, and have won Formidable Prizes themselves? Fearing to reveal incompetence as a reader, Z casts his lot with the experts, convinces himself that he loves A's book, and feels a lot better about himself.

Poets, like members of oppressed minorities, may also feel that they should not criticize each other. Mom's Dictum—"If you can't say some-

---

174 I use the term L=A=N=G=U=A=G=E poetry as shorthand for all "experimental" and extremely difficult poetry inspired by Marxist or other radical political theories.

thing nice, don't say anything at all"—often prevails. This makes practical sense, since the poetry world is small, poets' memories are long, and enemies may well have chances to strike back. But bad poetry—especially the difficult—is thereby given free rein.

Toward an Aesthetic Based on Evolutionary Psychology

Long before I knew the word *aesthetic*, taste fascinated me. Why did I love Kool-Aid when my parents didn't? Why did I like baseball and not basketball, while my friend Ted felt just the opposite? Why did "boobs" strike me as funny at nine, and beautiful at thirteen? Why did so many of my guitar students—who claimed to love, and in some cases, to *live* for music—have little feeling for anything but then-current hits?

Why, when I ask beginning poetry students to choose their favorite poem from the year's *Best American*, do they so often—on the second day of class, knowing nothing of my taste, and virtually nothing about poetry—pick the same three or four poems: often the three or four that I like best too? Why do I find so much lauded contemporary poetry to be lackluster, if not downright bad?

I know that postulating *natural human taste* is at odds with recent literary theory.[175] There is, as well, a potentially deterministic quality in evolutionary psychology that goes against my grain. Still, the Darwinian approach to aesthetics explains too many of my questions to ignore. Defining the poem as fitness indicator may not be concrete as a sidewalk, but it's less vaporous than the pure opinion that normally passes for critical judgment.

> Good Poem = Fitness Indicator = Aesthetically pleasing =
> 1. Admired as difficult-to-write AND
> 2. Perceived as successful = enjoyed

If a good poem must be 1. admired as difficult to write, and 2. enjoyed, "The Love Song of J. Alfred Prufrock" qualifies, for me, as a good poem. Eliot's brilliant imagery and innovative use of meter and rhyme, as well as the psychological depth and sheer beauty of the poem, far exceed the average poet's, let alone the average person's, ability. In addition, the poem

---

175 Steven Pinker demolishes that theory in *The Blank Slate: The Modern Denial of Human Nature*, cited above.

is reasonably accessible on one reading, improves with subsequent ones, and has been enjoyed by many readers over many years.

William Carlos Williams's "The Red Wheelbarrow" is a tougher case to make. On its surface, the poem looks too easy to write. Nor will it strike every reader as especially enjoyable. A common response of students on their first exposure to the poem is, "Why is that good?" or even, "Why is that a poem?"

"The Red Wheelbarrow" lacks Eliot's clear verbal brilliance. It seems plain and simple-minded, withholding nothing except the reason *why* "so much depends . . ." Readers must know about the poem's technical innovations (as of 1923), and understand how Williams uses line breaks for pacing, before the poem can be admired as at all difficult to write. Before it can be enjoyed as more than a trivial and puzzling note-to-the-self, readers must accept the poem as a kind of American haiku, celebrating the thing-ness of the world.

Another good test case is L=A=N=G=U=A=G=E poetry. A poem such as Ron Silliman's "Tjanting"—". . . A plausibility. Analogy to 'quick' sand. Mute pleonasm. Nor that either. Planarians, trematodes. Bookd burglar. What water was, wld be. Last week I cld barely write 'I grip this pen.' The names of dust . . ."[176]—may at first glance seem as difficult to write as to apprehend. Yet poems not unlike this one can be produced by mechanical means—the "cut up" method of arbitrary juxtapositions, for instance—or by using mathematical formulae (every tenth phrase, say, from arbitrarily chosen sources) to generate text. The parts of L=A=N=G=U=A=G=E poetry that probably *are* difficult to write—those parts that show wit, insight, irony, close observation, or what non-initiates might, in non-L=A=N=G=U=A=G=E poems, call evidence of *talent*—are precisely those parts that veer away from the pure indeterminacy of L=A=N=G=U=A=G=E poetry.

Silliman and some of his compeers are clearly bright; yet even if their poems *are* difficult to write, L=A=N=G=U=A=G=E poetry makes a poor fitness indicator, since its success as poetry is so difficult to judge. How can we assess a poem in which words and lines are interchangeable by design, where meaning is subverted along with standards of craft, and where co-responsibility for creating the poem rests with the reader, so bad

---

176 Ron Silliman, "Tjanting," *Postmodern American Poetry*, ed. Paul Hoover (New York: W.W. Norton & Company, 1994): 491.

poems are partially the reader's fault? The *poem*, like the *author*, *reader*, and the *self* itself, dissolve into the deconstructed breeze.

L=A=N=G=U=A=G=E poetry fares no better on the enjoyment test. For all the theorists' talk of training a new kind of reader, few have emerged. Roland Barthes's "jouissance" notwithstanding, most human brains have not evolved to enjoy *as poetry* what L=A=N=G=U=A=G=E poems provide.

In the interest of survival and reproduction, humans evolved in certain ways, and not in others. Male and female brains *could* be identical, as many theorists and cultural critics wish; but they are not. It *could* be as easy to teach a child to fear flowers as to fear spiders; but it is not. As a species, humans like chocolate; they don't like cyanide.

Blame *natural human taste*.

Twenty years after Tchaikovsky's *Violin Concerto* shocked the music world, people had come to love it. After a century of discordant "modern" symphonic music, it still sounds bad to most human ears. People naturally enjoy the sound of cardinal's singing, but don't enjoy fingernails on a chalkboard.

What Do People Enjoy in Poetry?

I've proposed that readers prefer poems that are moderately difficult to apprehend. But the perceived difficulty of any poem depends on who is reading it. Quicker and more sophisticated minds may raise the poetic bar. Still, for the sake of this argument, a "general reader" of poetry can be defined as an adult, somewhat above average in intelligence, literate but not a literary specialist,[177] and the possessor of *natural human taste*. This reader would probably enjoy the highbrow/lowbrow radio program *A Prairie Home Companion*, where poets Billy Collins and Sharon Olds have appeared,[178] and which is hosted by Garrison Keillor, editor of the anthology *Good Poems*.[179]

For a poem to be judged good by my general reader, it's not enough that the poem achieve the optimal difficulty level. The genuinely good poem must contain other elements that, over millennia, people have evolved to

---

177 Even if few "general readers" of poetry exist, they seem a better standard than elite readers, since their governing aesthetic will be less distorted by extra-poetry concerns.

178 Collins and Olds, two of the best-known, best-selling, and most widely enjoyed poets in the country, are also—not coincidentally, I think—frequently attacked by the elite.

179 Garrison Keillor, *Good Poems* (New York: Viking, 2002).

admire and enjoy. Not coincidentally, these elements seem to derive from the author's general vitality, making them fitness indicators too.

If, like good fiction, the poem has *drama*; *conflict*; a *problem to be solved*; and a *compelling, well-paced story*, that's for the good. Lacking these things, the poem must contain enough *exceptional images* and *striking thoughts* to make it stand out in a crowd. Average thoughts and images, however sincere, aren't enough.

A *high level of craft* is necessary, though not sufficient to make a poem good.

A good poem must deal with *subjects and characters that are important or intriguing to the reader*; or it must convince the reader of the importance or intrigue of its subjects and characters. It also helps if the poem *grabs the attention early*, enticing the reader in.

A good poem must provide sufficient payoff to justify the time and energy spent reading it. *Memorable language*; *fresh insights*; *vivid, vicarious experiences*; and *effective use of humor* can help with this payoff.

Since no poem can indicate fitness if the reader can't assess its quality, a good poem must be *understandable*. This means that *clarity* is important, too. Evasiveness, opacity, and muddled thinking are rarely virtues in a poem.

This doesn't mean there is no room for *mystery*. That quality can be very attractive in a poem, provided the mystery is genuine, and not mere mystification.[180] The nature of so-called *dark matter* is a genuine and fascinating mystery. The meaning of a garbled sentence or a willfully obscure stanza is not.

Reticence is an elite value that, Elizabeth Bishop aside, generally leads to pale, tame verse. "The folk" enjoy *energy*, *extravagance*, *variety*, *surprise*, *imagination*, *wildness*, *loud and flashy colors*, *passion*, and *wit*. When skillfully controlled, such qualities—found abundantly in Shakespeare—help to make a poem enjoyable and good.

Though some of the elite reject meaning, and may scorn even a provisional and subjective certainty, the "folk" look to poetry for, in Joseph Campbell's words, "myths to live by." They cite poems, as they cite proverbs, joke, and stories, to clarify complex life-issues. Good poetry, then, needs a *more-or-less determinable point or theme*, or at least a *not-too-ambiguous meaning*. Good poetry may even contain that much-ridiculed quality the folk call *wisdom*.

---

180 I'm not the first Creative Writing teacher to find that problem poems are frequently mysterious where they should be clear, and/or clear when they could use some mystery.

Since standards of propriety help to keep many truths out of sight and mind, *impropriety* can be an asset to a poem. So can *audacity* and *non-conformity*, if used in the service of determinable meaning. Though these qualities may shock some general readers, such readers may be more open-minded than the elite, with their predictable and rigid verities.

Pompous, precious, prim, preening, and politically correct poems, no matter their politics, won't make the grade. Indeterminacy and imperme-ability disqualify most poems, no matter how interesting the theory from which those qualities derive.

A poem may be noteworthy from a technical standpoint, but like a musical etude, fall short as art. Many respected journals are full of poems that, like conscientious students, dutifully grind through the approved contemporary paces with careful craft but no fire. They may deserve an A for effort, but not for poetry.

Weak-willed, fussy, and undistinguished poems don't make the grade as fitness indicators or as poems. Blasé, jaded, too-hip, excessively self-con-scious poems may succeed as social displays, but not as art.

A good poem must be written in a *convincing, appealing, unique,* and *compelling voice*—one with which the reader is happy to spend time. Con-temporary skepticism about "the self" can be incorporated into that voice, enriching it. But if such skepticism detracts from the appeal of the voice, or negates it, the poem won't be enjoyable, and therefore can't be good.

Like a good story, novel, or film, the poem must *seize the reader's in-terest*, and *hold on*. To do this, it can't be static, enervated, or inert; it must have a strong, forward-driving *energy*. It must (derided principle) *entertain*.

When Is Showing Off Just Showing Off?

If poetry is a fitness display, the poet has license to enjoy that display—to, as musicians do, "play." Beethoven was glad to show off his virtuosity as a pianist and composer; listeners were delighted to witness it. Good po-ems should rock like Zeppelin, caress like Chopin, fulminate like Rage Against the Machine, vamp like Queen, clown like Fats Waller, improvise like Charlie Parker, whisper like Debussy, roar like Motörhead.

Poets should feel free to indulge in displays of imagination, high spirits, stylistic panache, and verbal virtuosity—as long as such display is in the service of the reader and the poem. Hamlet's "To be or not to be" solilo-quy is not mere showing off, since Shakespeare is doing his best to com-municate to an audience something potentially important to that audience. His display is thrilling and not self-indulgent, in marked contrast to a poet whose display is in the service of Ego. Such a poet is concerned primarily with communicating his or her wonderfulness to the audience. "You should read this because I'm greater than you," the works of such a poet state.

A poet who loses control of a display is like a juggler who throws up too many balls. The poem comes crashing down.

Readers must guard, too, against fraudulent displays. This requires critical judgment. Still, if a good poem indicates fitness, we have something to guide that judgment. We can ask, "Did I enjoy this?" Then, "Does this show rare talent, vision, and skill, or just average ability?"

Using folk standards to define good poetry will favor less difficult poems. Yet good-but-difficult poems can still be appreciated for the fitness displays they are. Such poems will simply find a smaller audience: those readers for whom the poem, like a 300-pound bench press for a pro football lineman, is only moderately difficult. A poem that works on several levels, as Shakespeare's plays do, can provide maximum enjoyment for maximum numbers.

Simply by writing poetry, poets to some extent make themselves elite. To write well, though, they must be people before they are poets. Artists lose touch with folk aesthetics—natural human taste—at great peril to their work. However sophisticated and serious they may be, writers, readers, and scholars must not forget that poetry's main purpose is to give enjoyment; and the reader's, to receive it. For this to happen, poets must fully express their humanness. They must also possess, and express, exceptional vitality. Like Michelle Kwan skating, or Derek Jeter playing shortstop, they must feel completely free to strut their stuff. Poetry need not and should not be the intellectual hair shirt most Americans think that it is. It should be a coat of many colors—an energetic and glorious display, like a Rembrandt painting, a Bach cantata, a Cirque du Soleil trapeze act, an orange sunrise behind mountains full of birdsong.

The display called Poetry is not the poet's alone. The audience, as Understander, has a major part to play. Writers and readers share the pleasure of good poetry. It seems right that they share in the glory.

Back to the Narrative:
Breathing New Life into a Tired Form

"Am I irrelevant because I write narrative poems?" a friend asked last week, not rhetorically. The world of poetry is as fashion-conscious as the world of *haute couture*. Reputations wax and wane; poetic strategies do too. Ten years ago, I heard, "The lyric is dead." Now, de-sequenced and ironized, it has revived. The narrative, though—especially the short, first person kind—still scores low on the poetic hipness scale.

As Tony Hoagland explains in "Fear of Narrative and the Skittery Poem of Our Moment,"[181] narrative is, in some quarters, mistrusted as oppressive, over-controlling, even fascistic. "Systematic development and continuity are considered simplistic, claustrophobic, even unimaginative,"[182] Hoagland adds. "Obliquity, fracture, and discontinuity are in."[183] ". . . charisma belongs to the erratic and subversive."[184]

Progress and *closure*, viewed as illusory in life, are suspect in narrative, too. Ditto the concept of a consistent, definable "I."

Furthermore, because no narrative can tell "the whole story, some readers object to the smugness and presumption of the narration. 'Whose narrative is this?' they cry. 'Not mine!'"[185] In addition, Hoagland postulates a "fear of submersion, or enclosure"[186] that makes postmodern readers resist being swept away by narrative, losing "not consciousness perhaps, but self-consciousness"[187]—the type of awareness they most prize.

---

181 Tony Hoagland, "Fear of Narrative and the Skittery Poem of Our Moment," in *Real Sofistikashun* (Minneapolis: Graywolf Press, 2006).
182 Ibid., 174.
183 Ibid., 177.
184 Ibid.
185 Ibid.
186 Ibid.
187 Ibid., 178.

That the short narrative poem is so common lowers its status still more. Writing programs, presses, and periodicals confront mountains of poems chronicling events from childhood, the illness and death of relatives, and the general doings of the author's life. Short narratives-from-life seem to be what beginning poets write. When such poems are spoken by an "I," the story will all-too-likely be pedestrian, predictable, and "true," as in the hypothetical poem "Mama's Hands," summarized, with arbitrary line breaks, below.

> A middle-aged son comes to see his mother, who is in
> the hospital for a serious illness. Using first
> person, he meticulously describes walking through the hospital, and
> entering the room. He records
> small talk with his mother, just as it occurred.
> He feels guilty that he doesn't see
> her more. He describes the hospital room, and his
> mother's hands on the bedclothes. He
> recalls a time when she made cookies for him and his friends.
> Her hands were soft and young, and he took her cookies for
> granted. She made two kinds; he describes both, as well
> as all of his friends, taking care
> to name and comment on each one.
> He realizes that the cookies were made with love, which is
> essential to a good life. Squeezing his
> mother's hands, he promises to come back soon—i.e., before
> it is too late.

A poem about a parent's hands is not exactly virgin soil. Nor is the situation—adult child visits ailing parent—unfamiliar in contemporary life or poetry. The poem is originality-challenged from the start.

Chopping prose into lines won't add to the poem's music, or boost its cachet.

Description of the hospital will be overlong: many unfocused details instead of a few telling ones. The poem will describe because that's what poems do.

It will use banal dialogue because that's what the poet and his mother said. The poet thinks he owes it to his mom to tell *what really happened*. The feelings expressed may be unremarkable, but they are the feelings he had.

He'll see the hospital room as sterile, frighteningly cold, with just the sort of look, feel, smell that most of us would come up with if we had to describe such a room from distant memory. The poet may even allow some anger to escape in words like "cheap," "plastic," "second-rate," "impersonal."

His mother's hands will be "gnarled," "liver-spotted," or both. It's not important to the poem that she made two different kinds of cookies, but she did, and so the fact, along with the kinds of cookies, will be here. Ditto the friends. Good poems use specific details. And truth must be told.

The poet's insight at the end may not surprise even him; yet it will be deeply felt, he'll choke up each time he thinks of the scene. The poem will be sincere, heartfelt, accurate, and therefore, in our poet's mind, excellent by definition.

Readers may disagree. The problem, though, is not the short narrative form. Consider how many contemporary classic poems are short, first-person narratives drawn from real life. Elizabeth Bishop's "The Fish" and "In The Waiting Room," James Wright's "A Blessing," Gerald Stern's "The Dancing," plus any number of poems by Phil Levine, Sharon Olds, and "I do this I do that" Frank O'Hara, show how effective the approach can be.

The short narrative poem is, in part, a victim of its own success. In an age of "Make it new," literary careers are less often made by saying, "That was great! Do it again," than by declaiming (and supporting with impressive theory), "No! Wrong! You should be doing *this*." Add this nay-saying impulse to the problems described above, and it's no wonder that the field of short narrative poetry seems unpromising ground. For poets to give it up, though—as they have, for the most part, ceded longer narratives to prose—is to give up too much.

In any case, narrative can't be given up. The human brain, however clearly it may see the limits of the method, evolved to organize events in narrative terms. Narrative is how we make sense of, and survive in, the world. (Ogg was killed by a tiger over there. Don't go over there. If you do, watch out for tigers.)

Just as all narratives, if they are to be poems, must contain at least a hint of lyric, the purest lyric, to make sense, must at least imply a narrative. Blake's "The Tyger," for all its lyric beauty, implies two: the tiger's creation, and attack by the great cat.

The brain will force even a poem meant *not* to make sense to imply some narrative—that, or be treated as mere noise. Jonathan Doherty's "The Crossbones Are Comatose" is a case in point.

The crossbones are comatose,
the river flows clockwise. Paranoid,
calibrate with the parterre.

There's a Spaghetti inquest,
the exodus and spleen impose
the linkboys and autotypes.

. . .

Eldritch is larcenous,
teems when genocide possess,
presuming it's a menorah.[188]

This poem definitely "makes it new" with unexpected juxtapositions and arcane vocabulary. Some readers may enjoy it for its sound. Any reader, though, who wants to know what the poem *means* will likely impose some narrative.

The "crossbones are comatose" may imply that the picturesque, "Aar-rh"-spewing, much-romanticized Pirate—and by extension, Romance it-self—is no longer viable. Perhaps the river flows clockwise because, in our mechanized and soul-less age, even Huck Finn's Mississippi is constrained by the time-clock. Faced with such mind-killing restraint, the speaker has become understandably fearful of offending the Powers-That-Be, and therefore tries to *calibrate* his life like a Rolex watch—to make it more accurate, orderly, and aesthetically pleasing—to make it, in fact, like an ornamental garden in which the flowers and paths form a pattern, i.e., a parterre.

Given time, I could make the rest of the poem fit that story. So could you—or "discover" some narrative of your own. Drink deep, if that's your cup of tea.

Direct narrative, on the other hand, appeals innately to the human brain, with no extraordinary learning, no unusual taste, no special effort required. The short narrative poem remains a strong, graceful, and natu-ral strategy with the potential to reclaim for poetry some of the territory ceded to prose.

---

188 Jonathan Doherty, "The Crossbones Are Comatose," *La Petite Zine* (Fall 2004).

Allison Joseph's "Traitor" shows how effective the straightforward first-person narrative can still be.

Traitor

What did that girl on the playground mean
when she hissed *you ain't black* at me,

pigtails bouncing, her hands
on her bony hips? She sucked her teeth,

stared at me with such contempt
that I wanted to hide in my mother's

skirts, wanted to scurry to my house's
hall closet, safe among the great

dark coats. *You talk funny*, she said,
all proper, as if pronunciation

was a sin, a scandal, a strike
against the race only a traitor

would perform, an Uncle Tom sellout.
Somehow I'd let her down by not

slurring, I'd failed her by not
letting language laze on its own,

its sound unhurried. I'd said
isn't rather than *ain't*,

called my mother *mom* instead
of *momma*, pronounced *th* distinctly

so no one would confuse *them*
with *dem*, *those* with *dose*.

Your momma talk that funny?
the girl demanded, her face

in my face now, her nose
inches from mine, her eyes

lit by something near hate,
but more ferocious, a kind

of disgust mixed with pity,
disdain. *We're from Canada,*

I said, and the girl's eyes
went wide, as if I'd said

cantaloupe, or *harpoon*,
or some nonsense word like

*abracadabra. There must not be
no black folks in Canada then,*

she sneered, leaning in further,
pushing on my chest with one

bony finger, pinning me there
like a bug to a fly screen,

pressing me so hard that
my lower lip started to tremble

on its own, a sign of weakness.
She laughed a mocking, heavy

laugh, telling me *go on and cry,
white girl, cry till your momma*

can hear, pushing me so I toppled
onto my back, ripping the pants

> my mother warned me not to rip.
> She stood over me, laughing
>
> like she'd just seen the world's
> best clown, laughing though I
>
> was just as dark as she,
> my hair in the same
>
> nappy plaits, my skin
> the same rough brown.[189]

This poem uses vivid natural diction to tell a good story. The language does not scream, "Look! A poem!" Yet it does its job well, providing vivid details, plus believable, incisive dialogue. Whether or not the poem is autobiographical, nothing is extraneous, nothing left in because it "really happened."

The poem conveys and provokes strong emotion, providing unusual perspective on the often clichéd issue of race. When the bully stands in what she thinks is triumph over a girl who looks like her, we see that her "victim" is herself, brought down by her own self-hate. The drama unfolds and concludes as powerfully as a good short story, but more economically.

Like fiction, short narrative poems may use the second-person "you" or third-person limited to give the poem more distance from the poet, and to make the work seem less confessional, as in this poem by Jim Daniels.

> The Day After
>
> the worst snowstorm in years,
> a horn blares—a stuck cab
> blocks the street, the guy
> in the car behind leans on his horn
> then stomps out and starts pounding
> on the cabbie's door shouting move it
> move your fucking car and the cabbie's
> saying I'm stuck and the guy's screaming
> try it you're not stuck and the cabbie opens

---

189 Allison Joseph, "Traitor," in *Stand Up Poetry: An Expanded Anthology*, 164–66.

his door and the guy hits him in the face
and throws snow at him and the cabbie says
he's gonna call the cops and the guy says
call the cops fucking call the cops
and the cabbie says I'm gonna get my gun
and he goes around to his back door
and the other guy starts running
back to his car until it occurs to him
that the cabbie's bluffing because he's stopped
with his hand on his back door
so the guy charges back saying
get your gun get your fucking gun
but the cabbie don't move
because he ain't got a gun so the guy starts
throwing snow at him again and shouting
move, motherfucker, let's see your gun
but he ain't got no gun
so the guy keeps taunting him
let's see your fucking gun
and punches the cabbie in the face
then gets in his car and rear ends
the cab till it's out of his way
and speeds off and the cabbie's alone
in the street shouting next time
I'll have a gun
next time I'll have a fucking gun.[190]

A prose writer might take pages to accomplish what "The Day After" does in less than one. The fast pace evokes the attacker's hair-trigger temper and homicidal rage. That pace, along with the dialogue, convey excitement, immediacy, drama, and a strong sense of urban reality.

The poem does not belabor us with strained, "imaginative" language. It tells its story in the demotic, as it should. As for poetic devices—the whole poem is a metaphor for life in the city, and for that matter, the world. It pulses with aggressive energy. It flexes and rushes and rocks and wants to kill you. This is realism on steroids and crack.

---

190 Jim Daniels, "The Day After," *Poets of the New Century*, ed. Roger Weingarten and Richard M. Higgerson (Boston: David R. Godine, 2001): 47.

Some poets, while not abandoning the narrative, add freshness and interest to their poems by exploring dreams and the fantastic. James Tate is
famous for this type of narrative. Richard Garcia's "Why I Left the Church"
begins realistically, then floats up into pure imagination.

Why I Left the Church

Maybe it was
because the only time
I hit a baseball
it smashed the neon cross
on the church across
the street. Even
twenty-five years later
when I saw Father Harris
I would wonder
if he knew it was me.
Maybe it was the demon-stoked
rotisseries of purgatory
where we would roast
hundreds of years
for the smallest of sins.
Or was it the day
I wore my space helmet
to catechism? Clear plastic
with a red and white
inflatable rim.
Sister Mary Bernadette
pointed toward the door
and said, "Out! Come back
when you're ready."
I rose from my chair
and kept rising
toward the ceiling
while the children
screamed and Sister
kept crossing herself.
The last she saw of me

was my shoes disappearing
through cracked plaster.
I rose into the sky and beyond.
It is a good thing
I am wearing my helmet,
I thought as I floated
and turned in the blackness
and brightness of outer space.
My body cold on one side and hot
on the other. It would
have been very quiet
if my blood had not been
rumbling in my ears so loud.
I remember thinking,
Maybe I will come back
when I'm ready.
But I won't tell
the other children
what it was like.
I'll have to make something up.[191]

Even further removed from the basic first-person short narrative poem is the fantastical prose-poem. Russell Edson's "The Retirement of the Elephant" tells how a circus elephant, after a lifetime of hard work, retires to "a small cottage on a quiet street" to spend its last years in tranquility, preparing for "the coming collapse of the biology."

Alas, the elephant's size is a problem. Unable to squeeze through his front door of his small cottage, he smashes his way in, whereupon the floor collapses and he falls into the cellar. Finding the back door as tiny the front, the elephant breaks it down, then levels all of his remaining walls.

Now the elephant realizes that its only course is to
run amuck—Yes, just to run amuck!
Goddamn everything![192]

---

191 Richard Garcia, "Why I Left the Church," in *Stand Up Poetry: An Expanded Anthology*, 109–10.
192 Russell Edson, "The Retirement of the Elephant," in *The Intuitive Journey and Other Works*, (New York: Harper & Row, 1976): 177.

Edson's novel-in-half-a-page appeals on many levels. Its sincere, hard-working elephant captures the reader's interest and sympathy. Anyone who has ever scrimped and sacrificed to no avail—anyone who has trusted the wisdom of his culture and/or "superiors," done what she was told, served faithfully, then received the Green Weenie—will resonate with Edson's metaphor.

A narrative poem may, like a novel, jump back and forth in time. Brigit Pegeen Kelly's "Song"[193] begins with a goat's head, cut off and hung in a tree, singing. The poem flashes back to the boys who killed the goat; then to the head pulling the heart out of the goat's body; then to the heart singing from the goat's head. We learn, next, that the goat belonged to a little girl, who loved it. Then we learn how the girl sensed that the goat had been harmed, even before people found the body by the railroad tracks, then the head in its tree. We learn how people hid the goat's body to spare the girl, gathered money to buy her a new goat, and found the guilty boys. We flash back again to the boys killing the goat, then forward into the boys' future, the goat never ceasing to sing, year after year, torturing them with its "sweet" song.

Suffused with the dream-like quality of fairy tales, "Song" would be a good story, even if told chronologically. By moving back and forth in time, Kelly conveys a sense of timelessness, complicating and deepening the narrative with lyric mystery.

A skillful poet may add power and complexity to a poem by combining narratives. In "A Story,"[194] by Susan Mitchell, a story of the speaker in a Chicago bar blends into a story of the speaker in a New York bar, which moves into a story of psychic surgery, followed by a story of walking home from the New York bar, then a story of a walk in Chicago, then a story of a fatal knife fight in the Chicago bar, followed by what, we realize at last, the whole poem has led up to: the story of a transfusion the speaker received at age nineteen, which caused her great pain, but saved her life. The poem is an extended *thank you*, each story adding resonance, each pitching in to create an ending of great power and dramatic punch.

Poets may combine the power of narrative with the power of lyric in what we might as well call *lyric narrative*. My favorite example of this, Dylan Thomas's "Fern Hill," is too well known to require discussion here.

---

193 Brigit Pegeen Kelly, *Song*.
194 Susan Mitchell, "A Story," in *Rapture* (New York: Harper Perennial, 1992): 38–40.

Suffice it to say that, in language of great beauty, Thomas tells the story of a boy's life on a Welsh farm.

B. H. Fairchild, in "Body and Soul,"[195] gives us *narrative-plus-meditation*. A fascinating story about fifteen-year-old Mickey Mantle used as a "ringer" in a baseball game, teams up with a meditation on—among other things—manhood, blasted dreams, hopelessness, spiritual wealth and poverty, and "the vast gap between talent and genius."

Both the story *and* the meditation could have powered first-rate poems. Together, they make a masterpiece—not over-long at 110 lines, though too long to quote here.

Finally, we come to the sort of narrative poem—not always short—for which both Albert Goldbarth and David Kirby are best known. Both poets complicate their narratives by interweaving multiple stories, meditations, and facts—throwing in anything, including the kitchen sink, that interests them. I'll call them, for the purposes of this paper, *kitchen sink narratives*.[196]

Kirby's "The House of Blue Light"[197]—125 lines long—starts when "Little Richard comes on the TV at Gold's Gym / and the first thing that happens is, I burst into tears." This leads to a story of French historian Fustel de Coulanges, then cuts back to an extended story of Little Richard and Katie Couric on the *Today Show*, which moves into a quasi-comic meditation on manhood, then to a conversation with the speaker's wife about his son's going off to college, then a brief meditation on the link between pop music and sentiment, then a story about the death of Roy Orbison, and Roy's singing of "Danny Boy," and the story contained in "Danny Boy," followed by a vision of his son dressed as Danny Boy, then a brief excursion into Little Richard's "House of Blue Light," then a discussion of the strange goings-on in Muhammad Ali's "near room," then comments on the pronouncing of "expedition" by an Italian biologist who went to Antarctica, then the story of a game called "African Ranger," then a story of the day the speaker and his brother helped his elderly parents leave the family home, the father weeping, the sons depressed, then the speaker imagining a journey through the woods to the House of Blue Light, which sounds a lot like heaven.

---

195 B. H. Fairchild, "Body and Soul," in *Stand Up Poetry: An Expanded Anthology*, 96–98.
196 Goldbarth's book of new and selected poems is titled *The Kitchen Sink* (Graywolf Press, 2009).
197 David Kirby, "The House of Blue Light," in *The House on Boulevard St.: New and Selected Poems* (Baton Rouge: Louisiana State University Press, 2007): 115–18.

The fact that Kirby can fit all of this into a poem that manages to be entertaining, informative, exhilarating, funny, and very moving all at the same time, shows the power of this narrative approach in the right hands.

In addition to these approaches to narrative, we can add at least two more that grow out of postmodern reservations about narrative. The first of these, which I will call the *narrative of exhaustion*, uses narrative to comment on the impossibility of writing good narratives these days. Mark Halliday is a master of this approach. His poem "The Ivory Novel"[198] summarizes a novel the speaker considers writing, but decides not to. "Credentials"[199] lists standard narrative scenarios full of drama and suffering—loss of a child, rape, parental battery, service in Vietnam—while simultaneously questioning the authority of any writer who has not experienced such things, and satirizing the idea of the poet-who-has-suffered. Contemporary life is seen as simply too boring, too generic, too clichéd, too dispassionate (or its passion too subjective and ludicrous) to fuel traditional narrative.

Mock-narrative poetry uses the form of narrative to mimic and to ironize. In mock narrative, the conventions of story—this happened; then that happened—create a clothesline on which to hang what really matters to the poet: irony, wit, intelligence, imaginative flights, literary sophistication, lyricism, off-kilter vision, and frequently, the conveying of anxiety, sadness, and world-weariness, as in "The Mauvais Gondolier" by Cole Heinowitz, excerpted below.

> As we sat in Central Park
> you turned my head to see
> what I'd already heard.
> It was the *mauvais gondolier*
> and his baritone rang
> through the trees from across
> the pond. Melancholy, yes.
> Even manful—but oh,
> there was no life in the man! . . .

---

198 Mark Halliday, "The Ivory Novel," in *Selfwolf* (Chicago: The University of Chicago Press, 1999): 47–49.
199 Ibid., 9.

A cardinal in the bay leaves
that looked like bamboo
was gone when I turned but
the gondolier sang on, just to say
he was numb to the pain of it all.
Your hands reach my waist, I
remember this place as rowboats
float over green water
and never a gondolier's sigh.[200]

Conclusion

It can be tempting to dismiss the short narrative poem today. What intelligent reader can doubt that language sometimes fails to communicate?—that "I" can be a slippery customer?—that narrative imposes an order that the real world (whatever *that* is) partly or completely lacks? Who doesn't distrust authority, and any number of once-revered verities?

Who wants to be a throwback/reactionary/troglodyte—neither hip, "with it," culturally high-end, nor on the cutting edge? What contemporary poet, reading Pound, Eliot, and Stevens in college, didn't wish to make vatic pronouncements that would be interpreted and reinterpreted by sophisticated professionals—to be a genius with thoughts and perceptions too fine, nuanced, complex, profound to be conveyed by direct statement or simple narrative?

Since so few people read poetry, why risk being dissed by your peers for taking an un-cool approach? Why miss out on Po-Biz perquisites? Why risk telling a story that people can understand, and that could reveal you as unexceptional, unoriginal, just like everybody else? Why leave your naked self nowhere to hide?

B. H. Fairchild argues that good poetry helps us to experience the mystery of our own Being by connecting to the body, bringing the physicality of experience into language, "words proximate to the body, and the body of the world."[201] And what is more natural to the human body—to the human brain—than narrative?

John Fowles's *The French Lieutenant's Woman*, written forty-plus years ago, shows the power of an old-fashioned yarn to submerge readers

---

200 Cole Heinowitz, "The Mauvais Gondolier," *Fence* 10, no. 1 & 2 (2007).
201 B. H. Fairchild, "A Way of Being: Some Observations on the Ends and Means of Poetry," *New Letters* (Fall 2007).

in a narrative that lets them lose self-consciousness, even when the author continually breaks in to say, "Hey—this is fiction!"

Nor, on close examination, are other anti-narrative/anti-meaning arguments convincing. Language does not fail to communicate. For the most part, it communicates quite well, or you would not be reading this.

It's true that no one's identity is set in stone. Still, most of the traits that make up a personality—an "I"—are present in early childhood, and stay remarkably consistent over time.

That a given narrative is told from only one point of view does not make it false, but merely not-universal. Newton's Laws are not useless because they aren't absolute.

Progress may lack the quality of moral excellence with which it used to be invested; still, it does exist. People begin as babies, and "progress" from there. And how can closure be a myth to thinking creatures who inevitably die?

Far from being limited by these considerations, narrative can help us to more effectively consider them. Human beings turn to art to feel and understand more intensely. But especially to feel. Emotion is the strongest evidence of being. I feel, therefore I am. I feel, therefore I want to be.

Other artists envy musicians because, more directly than any other art, music makes us feel. Second only to music in that sphere is narrative. Combining a good story with the sounds of poetry gives us an artform that can approach the emotional directness and power of music. The problem is to come up with the good story, and then, to write it well.

It's hard to overemphasize the importance of stories to the human brain. We learn about the world and other people in two ways: through personal experience, and through stories told by other people. The stories we tell about ourselves show how we want others to see us. The stories we tell ourselves about ourselves help us determine who we are.

To give up narrative, then, is to give up much of poetry's power not only to illuminate, but to *embody* our humanness and our Being. It's also to lose out on much enjoyment, excitement, and fun.

Rather than rely on a dissembling style to seem original, why not do the work necessary to *be* so—the same work good writers have always done?

1. Observe the world closely, through the consciousness that is yours alone.
2. Experience the world fully, through that same consciousness.

3. Develop and support that consciousness.
4. Reflect cogently on what you have observed and experienced, as well as on your consciousness.
5. Find words and forms that will, with clarity, convey 1–4 to others.

This simply can't be done without narrative.

Why not embrace, then, what you can't help but do? When narrative comes knocking, don't send it away. Don't fear to be seen with it, or to bring it home with you. At the very least, place it back in your poetic tool box. Who knows what good things it may do for you?

Where I Stand

Of the bewildering number of styles into which American poetry has split, I'd guess I'm linked most closely with the Stand Up kind. Stand Up, though, has never been an organized school of poetics, nor do Stand Up poets write only Stand Up poems. Fewer than half of my own poems would qualify. Still, I'm a strongly reader-centered poet. Critical theory aside, I believe that meaning and clear communication are both possible and desirable. I hope to entertain and, possibly, enlighten readers, as other poets have entertained and enlightened me.

Right now I'm especially drawn to poems of wild imagination and unexpected associations. I'm fascinated by the unconscious mind. I want to give readers new experiences, not just to help them relive old ones. I like to satirize and celebrate—sometimes both at the same time. I'm drawn to investigate, and sometimes celebrate, "ugly" emotions: anger, vengefulness, envy, selfishness, schadenfreude. Why celebrate only "nice" things?"

Having grown up a closeted agnostic in a Methodist church, a delinquent in the guise of honor student, I resent pomposity and poppycock. So much wisdom and knowledge proves unwise and untrue. I want my poems to be truth-tellers and bullshit-busters.[202]

I love energetic poems that boil, seethe, flash, or shimmer on the page. I made my living as a rock singer/guitarist for years, and approach my poems—even the sad ones—with rock-and-roll fervor. Too many poems lie on the page as if they've been chloroformed.

I'm drawn to humor for the fun of it, and for its seriousness. Many of my happiest and most profound childhood experiences involved laughing with family and friends. Humor is quintessentially human, and intensely

---

202 This means that I believe there is a truth, however subjectively defined.

subversive. It's also one of the great forces of redemption in human life, lifting our spirits as it brings us the bad news.[203]

Humor is also a great way to deal with postmodern concerns—slipperiness of language and identity, tendency of statements to deconstruct themselves, etc.—while not driving the reader catatonic. Comedy, I state in *Stand Up Poetry*, "is ideally suited to capture the absurdities, enormities, and pathos of modern life." It's compatible, too, with deep emotion and tenderness—areas I continue to explore.

I enjoy poems in fixed form, and even write a few myself.

I've never competed in a Slam, though I've had several students on the CSU Long Beach Slam Team. I applaud their energy, and warn them that improving the literary quality of their poems probably won't help them win Slams.

I'm interested in the ideas of L=A=N=G=U=A=G=E poetry and its offshoots, but less interested in the poems. I'm not convinced that human minds work the way L=A=N=G=U=A=G=E theorists think they do. Strategies of monotony and repetition don't kick my mind into new ways of reading or perceiving. Boredom does not enlighten me; it drives me away. Nor am I interested in doing more than the usual co-creating with the poet. I'm well aware how commerce co-opts language, but don't believe that being hard to understand is the best way to counter this.

Still, I could be wrong, and certainly don't begrudge other poets their interests or experiments. I'd love to see a larger audience for poetry, and believe that the kind I espouse is more likely to attract it; but I no longer believe that poetry will become even one-tenth as popular as rock-and-roll.

When asked to state my poetics for "Poet of the Month," a website housed at Vanderbilt University, I sent an early version of this, by which I still stand:

I like poems that generate momentum, and hit hard.

I like poems that crackle with energy—even despairing energy. I don't like poems that droop with world-weariness.

I like to hear voices I've never heard before.

I like to see from fresh perspectives, through fascinating eyes.

I like poems that renew not just the language, but the world. Imagination is an end in itself.

---

203 Think of the Monty Python song in *Life of Brian*: "Always Look on the Bright Side of Life," as sung by convicts on the cross.

I like strangeness, unless it's gratuitous, or not gratuitous enough. (Monty Python's "Fish Dance" is gratuitous enough.)

I don't like poems that won't risk meaning.

I don't like poems that ring my doorbell and run.

I don't like monotonous poems, even when the one note is a good one.

I don't like poems that use their lines like well-made bricks tossed at random on a lawn; these poems never get off the ground.

I don't like poems that want to show off more than they want to talk to me.

I don't like poems that think they're better than me.

I like to be swept up, carried away.

I like to laugh.

I don't exactly like to cry, but I like poems that make me want to (unless it's from frustration).

I like to be moved.

I like to be entertained.

I read for pleasure; struggling rarely pleases me.

I'm willing to work hard reading a poem, but what I get out of it must be worth more than the effort I put in. I want a fair return on my investment.

I don't like obscurity for its own sake—or, normally, for any other's.

I like language masterfully used: "the best words in the best order." Great language is necessary but not sufficient for great poetry.

I like words that are fun to say.

I love good metaphors.

I don't believe that "progress" occurs in poetry, but I try to write as if it does. I care more about progress in understanding the human psyche than in technical "advances."

I shy away from writing called "experimental"; the term usually sticks to failed experiments.

All good writing is experimental.

A poem is like the proverbial shark: if it stops moving forward, it dies. Also, a strong one can eat you alive.

The cardinal sin of poetry, and all art, is to bore.

I try to follow the Golden Rule, and write for others as I'd have them write for me.

A Musician Considers the Music of Poetry

I still remember my embarrassment when, in my first creative writing class, I asked the teacher to define "music" in poetry.

"If you have to ask," his sigh proclaimed, "you'll never know."

With apologies to Louis Armstrong, that's not a good answer. My teacher, to his credit, didn't leave the matter there. He launched into a paean to rhyme, meter, assonance, consonance, alliteration, and especially the "good ear," an organ that, judging from his reverent tone, could only be attained through divine grace.

I nodded, as if to say, "Yes. Just what I thought." But as the class progressed, it became clear that, many times, my teacher's ear and mine did not agree.

I was twenty-two, had been a professional musician for six years, and would make my living that way for seven more. My teacher, judging from his performance of several "Songs of Innocence," could not carry a tune. If one of us had a tin ear, which could it be?

I was out of grad school before I understood that, applied to poetry, the term *music* is mainly a metaphor.

Poetry shares many terms with music—*meter, beat, accent, rhythm, song, lyric, clunker, ear* (*tin* and *good*)—but the terms don't share definitions. In some cases, the difference is subtle; in others, extreme. All cases add to the confusion.

So does the fact that many poets feel themselves to be musicians manqué. The fine and musical poet Robert Wrigley laments, "I should have been a pair of vocal cords scatting across a bandstand somewhere."[204] Ezra Pound composed an opera (though his friend William Carlos Williams swore that Pound was tone-deaf). Robert Pinsky and B. H. Fairchild were serious students of the sax.

---

204 Robert Wrigley, "Making Music of Sense," *The Writer's Chronicle* (May 2000).

Think how often to write poetry is called to "sing," and how many poems are titled "Song," despite the fact that English poetry has not commonly been sung for centuries.

"Come my songs, let us express our baser passions," Pound declaims in "Further Instructions," though he was trying to move poetry away from the song-like prettiness of Edwardian poetry.

Music and poetry both make pleasing sounds. Music, though, can do its work with sound alone. Poetry needs help from meaning.

"I envy the musician's utter abandon to sound," Robert Wrigley states. "I want to be able to bring forth the very kind of exquisite sadness the music proffers, without the vast complications that attend when one cannot simply say, but must of course say *something*."[205]

Music's rhythm and melody act so strongly and directly on the body and emotions[206] that music has been likened to a drug. Poetry, on the other hand, consists of words, which carry meaning first, and only secondarily, rhythm and maybe some slight melody. These secondary qualities work as a minimal music; but most of poetry's effects are mediated by the intellect.

Take away the words from a good song, and the melody will please almost as much.[207] Remove the melody from most songs, and the words are diminished, often fatally.

Still, the opinion persists that verbal music is enough to make great art. A statement often heard in poetry circles—"I don't know what it means, but I love how it sounds"—may be true, but is misleading. Yes, words without meaning may please the ear. But a poem composed of them is like a boxer who polkas around the ring: amusing at best, and only for a little while.

Hearing poems in a foreign language is a good test of the Music Trumps Meaning doctrine. Some people claim to enjoy that experience enormously. Most, I suspect, react as I do, enjoying the alien sounds at first, then, as the novelty wears off, becoming bored. Not speaking Russian, I much prefer to hear Tchaikovsky than Akhmatova. If I want to revel in pure sound, I'll play guitar, turn on the stereo, or sit outside and listen to a mockingbird.

---

205 Wrigley, "Making Music of Sense."

206 Physiologically, of course, they work on the brain—but not that part of the brain which controls the conscious mind: the intellect.

207 When I couldn't understand recorded words while learning cover songs in my bands, I used to substitute nonsense syllables, with no lessening of the songs' appeal to audiences.

Poe's "The Bells" is as much a poem of pure sound as I know. Even its subject is sound.

> ... How they tinkle, tinkle, tinkle,
> In the icy air of night!
> While the stars that oversprinkle
> All the heavens seem to twinkle
> With a crystalline delight ...

The poem sonically evokes sleigh bells, marriage bells, alarm bells, and funeral bells. Yet the effect would be much lessened if the listener did not understand English.

Lewis Carroll's "Jabberwocky" revels in English-sounding words without dictionary meaning.

> 'Twas brillig, and the slithy toves
> > Did gyre and gimble in the wabe;
> All mimsy were the borogoves
> > And the mome raths outgrabe ...

I love the poem; but if it went on for pages, it would pall.

A few more music-to-poetry comparisons are worth keeping in mind.

Music can be made on many instruments. Poetry uses only the human voice (or, more commonly, words printed on a page). Next to music, its sonic resources are few.

Music makes use of pitches spanning several octaves, and degrees of loudness ranging from softer than pianissimo to the actual roar of a cannonade. Poetry, unless it's sung, changes pitch only slightly, and can't go softer than a whisper, or louder than a scream. Again, compared to music, poetry's sound is limited.

The rhythmic possibilities of poetry and music are both considerable. Their effect, though, is not the same.

Most Western music conforms to musical meter, with a fixed number of beats per measure.[208] This produces a strong, often danceable, rhythmic drive.

---

208 The number is generally three or four, with two, six, or eight beats per measure appearing less frequently. Other numbers of beats per measure, or varying numbers of beats per measure, are unusual.

Poetic meter involves a fixed number of accents per line, and a roughly fixed number of non-accents, arranged in a pattern of more or less regular "feet." Such poetry may possess strong rhythm, but rarely moves people to get up and dance.

By emphasizing musical meter (which may require accenting words differently from normal speech), "rap" and other styles of oral/performance poetry approach music's rhythmic intensity. Yet rappers still use rhythm instruments—anything from finger snaps to entire rock bands—to give their work more punch.

Words composed according to musical meter—song lyrics, nursery rhymes, rap, etc.—may vary a good deal in syllables-per-measure, and often seem irregular when scanned according to standard principles of poetic meter.

A poetic scansion of these words (to the tune of Chuck Berry's "Nadine") might look like this:

Standin' / in the rain, / what a pret / ty kit / ty cat, (Five poetic feet: trochaic, anapestic, anapestic, iambic, iambic)

but he / was cat / er waul / in' like / a girl / a boy / called fat. (Seven poetic feet: pyrrhic, iambic, iambic, pyrrhic, iambic, iambic, spondee)

The musical reading is much different.

Standin' in the rain, what	(six syllables, four accents, four musical beats)
a pretty kitty cat, but he	(eight syllables, four accents, four musical beats)
was cat-er-waulin' like	(six syllables, four accents, four musical beats)
a girl a boy called fat. (Rest)	(six syllables, four accents, four musical beats)

I can't speak Chuck's lines in their $\frac{4}{4}$ musical meter without feeling my body keep time. It's an autonomic response to the strong, consistent beat—like getting goosebumps in the cold.

Some poets claim that the rhythm of poetry—especially the iambic foot—is the rhythm of the heart: ba-dump, ba-dump. Certainly, a poem's rhythm adds to its emotional impact. But what makes your heart beat faster: the rhythms of "Ode to a Nightingale" or those of Beethoven's *Fifth*? Of "The Second Coming," or *The Rite of Spring*?

When traditionally metered verse mimics a musical beat, it may accentuate the musical limitations of verse. Theodore Roethke's much-loved "My Papa's Waltz," for instance, attempts to suggest a waltz by using a three beat line: iambic trimeter.

> The whiskey on your breath
> Could make a small boy dizzy;
> But I hung on like death:
> Such waltzing was not easy.

Robert Wallace, whose excellent book *Writing Poems*[209] I've often used in my classes, speaks of these lines as "wonderfully waltzing." But a waltzing meter would require dactylic feet. ("Ladybird, ladybird, fly away home ..." <u>One</u> two three, <u>one</u> two three, <u>one</u> two three, etc.) The musical effect Roethke produces is not of ¾ waltz time, but ⁴/₄ common time, with a one-beat rest after the last word of each line. "My Papa's Waltz" may be fine poetry, but it's not a waltz at all.

Free verse is frequently compared to jazz, since both can be free-flowing and improvisational. But most jazz has a consistent musical meter, producing sympathetic movement in the body, and making the music at least marginally danceable. In free verse, the language lacks a regular beat. Every line may have, in essence, a different Time Signature. This is like having none at all.

To note these differences between music and the music of poetry does not diminish the importance of sound in poetry. I agree with Kenneth Koch that poetry is a special language in which the sound of words has equal importance with their meaning. Effective use of sound is what turns language into poetry. There is no harm in calling these sounds "music"—if the music/poetry distinction is clear.

Yet even if poetry were identical to music, there would be more to the music of poetry than the "sweet sounds" with which the term is usually associated. Bach, Mozart, Tchaikovsky, Stravinsky, Schönberg, Irving Berlin, Duke Ellington, Charlie Parker, the Beatles, Queen, Nine Inch Nails, the Butthole Surfers, and Cannibal Corpse all make different kinds of music. Richard Wilbur, Tess Gallagher, David St. John, Dorianne Laux, William Trowbridge, Lynn Emanuel, Edward Hirsch, Brigit Pegeen Kelly,

---

209 Robert Wallace, *Writing Poems* (New York: HarperCollins, 1996).

Thomas Lux, David Shumate, Patty Seyburn, Charles Bukowski, and Susan Mitchell make different poetic music, too.

While I played music professionally, I wrote few mellifluous poems. In retrospect, I think this was because music seemed the better medium for my lyrical feelings. I preferred poems that were gritty and/or surreal and/or comic and/or narrative, and that sounded like real speech. The contemporary poets I most admired avoided rhyme, alliteration, meter—anything that called attention to their sound.

Still, all spoken language has sound, and thus, a kind of music. The music may be unformed and inept. It may be so bad it hurts. But just as some music intentionally jars and grates, poems may jar and grate on purpose, too.

The key question concerning music in poetry is always this: Given the words' purpose, *Do they sound right? Do they sound good?*

Since objective answers in the arts are hard to come by, we must fall back on informed subjectivity. That's where the "good ear" comes in.

A good ear in music means an unfailing sense of rhythm, and great sensitivity to pitch and harmony. These traits can be tested objectively.

Sensitivity to pitch and harmony, however, has little relevance to poetry. A good poetic ear requires sensitivity to the sound of words and the way they interact with—and influence—meaning. This is an aesthetic sense, and can't be verified objectively. Just as one concert violinist may prefer Vivaldi, another Prokofiev, two gifted poets may differ on what most pleases the ear.

Inborn talent aside, the vital element in attaining a good ear is practice. Reading, listening, and speaking, people with good poetic ears absorb the sounds of their native tongue, and learn the effects that are possible with it—learn them so well that these effects appear in their writing as if instinctively.

Poets also benefit from knowledge of traditional poetic devices. Forced to parrot definitions, students rarely see these devices' relevance. Yet, in the pop culture these children love, the devices are everywhere—used to give pleasure, and above all, to induce people to buy.

Advertisers must make optimal use of small amounts of time costing large amounts of money. If their message is in words, they must be, for their purpose, "the best words in the best order." This is, of course, Coleridge's definition of poetry.

A brief sampling of commercials will provide many examples of rhyme, meter, alliteration, assonance, consonance, anaphora, etc. The writers use these devices, not because they are students of poetry, but because the results sound good, and help to make their product seem appealing.

A frequent criticism of contemporary poetry is that it is merely prose chopped into lines. There's truth to this—and untruth, depending on the poet.

Many excellent contemporary poets use the language of ordinary speech. Their poems, therefore, sound very close to prose. Their special—i.e., musical—qualities are subtle. On the other hand, imagery—which contributes substantially to our perception of verbal music—may be especially memorable in speech-oriented poetry.

Many contemporary poets enhance the music of their free verse with ghost meters, suggesting more formal metrics by a preponderance of metered (usually iambic) feet.[210] Prose tends to contain many more unstressed than stressed syllables. Poetry, on the other hand, generally employs more stressed syllables. Textbook iambic, for instance, is fifty percent stressed syllables. The compression of poetry derives in part from the relatively high ratio of stressed to unstressed syllables.

The ghost (sometimes not-so-spectral) of iambic meter underlies the speech-oriented music of this poem by William Trowbridge.

Sticky Notes

They tell us to pay the bills, water
the begonias, wish Aunt Estelle
(the old bat) a happy eighty-sixth.
Our need accrues as years go by
and memory totters. We slap them
on the fridge, car keys, toothbrush,

though sometimes we can't tell
what the hell we wrote on them.

Near the final chill, we stick them
on birds and trees—goldfinch,
chickadee, sugar maple, weeping

---

210 Since iambic feet are common in everyday English, this can be done quite unobtrusively.

> birch, but they come unstuck,
> swirl away, muddled among
> the snow geese and brown leaves.[211]

Of the twenty-six syllables in the first three lines of this poem, thirteen—fifty percent—are accented, as would be the case in strict pentameter. Trowbridge's use of internal rhyme and assonance, though unobtrusive, adds to the impact of this powerful, understated poem.

The iambic beat of David St. John's "Memphis," by contrast, is so pronounced as to be much more than a ghost-meter.

> Sometimes when I'm bored by my own sins
>
> I slip on my old falcon helmet
> & drive the still glistening pink chariot
> Beyond these lonely gates of grace
>
> & down into the land the books call Memphis.[212]

In addition to strong iambics, there is a lot of alliteration and assonance even in this brief excerpt. The language goes beyond purely natural speech with phrases such as "glistening pink chariot," and metaphors such as "lonely gates of grace." The exotic locale and sense of grandeur-in-decay also contributes to St. John's characteristic music.

"The sound must seem an echo to the sense," Alexander Pope famously proclaims in "An Essay on Criticism." Few poets would disagree. Still, confusion abounds as to what Pope's dictum means in practice.

Many students believe that a given sound device must lead inevitably to a given effect. I've read that short lines move quickly, and also that they move slowly. I've been told that long lines move in a slow, stately manner—and that they move in a manic rush.

A preponderance of accents are believed to create, all by themselves, a slow and weighty movement of the line, as in these lines by Pope:

> When Ajax strives some rock's vast weight to throw,
> The line too labors, and the words move slow.

211 William Trowbridge, *Vanishing Point* (Pasadena: Red Hen Press, 2017).
212 David St. John, *The Red Leaves of Night* (New York: HarperCollins, 1999): 29.

Change the words, though, while keeping all accents the same, and different music can arise.

> When Irving strives some girl's pink cheek to kiss,
> His wet lips quiver as the town wits hiss.

Robert Wrigley describes[213] how Richard Hugo uses vowels and consonants to recreate the movement of a trout. Wrigley's reading is sensitive and perceptive. But would the identical sounds still evoke a trout if the subject were, say, a submarine sandwich?

"Of course not," Wrigley would be the first to say. But such demonstrations lead many students to believe that "music" can be created in such a recipe-like way. To become a good poet, then, one would need only to know what every English sound evokes, then use it accordingly.

The fact is, of course, that it's the combination of sound and meaning that creates poetry. Music and meaning are inseparable. Sound and sense.

"Okay, so music and poetry aren't identical," a friend said, after—fueled by several drinks—I'd expounded my thesis at some length. "What's the big deal?"

In all sobriety, it's this: As long as poets believe their primary job is to "make music," to "sing," they won't be playing to the real strengths of their art. And, I believe, they will be disappointed when, unlike what plays on the radio, their "music" does not move people to the depths and in the numbers that, deep down, they think it should.

Compared to music, poetry is a cerebral art—even when words seem to surge out of the body like high C out of Pavarotti's chest. "The language itself is the body's production, a sensual thing, the body's enactment of the mind's desire," Robert Wrigley says.[214] I wholeheartedly agree. But the singer's voice, rising from his heart, seems to leap straight to the hearts of his audience. Emotion evokes emotion, directly and without intercession by the conscious mind.

Words, on the other hand, however "musical," must be translated into meaning before they fully affect the heart.

We can hear favorite musical pieces many times, with virtually undiminished response. This is less true for favorite poems—especially free-verse poems. Our admiration for a poem may increase with exposure,

213 Wrigley, "Making Music of Sense."
214 Ibid.

but our physical response diminishes. The brain habituates to ideas more quickly than to emotions or body sensations. And poems, much more than music, are idea-based. We can enjoy sex or chocolate again and again. We devour ideas, assimilate them, and move on.

Every art has its strengths and weaknesses. No poem can paint as vivid a picture as Cézanne. But not even Rembrandt can portray the psyche as fully as Eliot does in "The Love Song of J. Alfred Prufrock."

No poem can evoke the pure, sweet melancholy of the adagio movement in Mendelssohn's *Violin Concerto*. But no music can teach us about love with the insight and mental dexterity of Donne's "A Valediction: Forbidding Mourning."

Compared to the direct emotional onslaught of music or visual arts, poetry works by indirection. Still, its strengths are formidable. And underlying all of them—coloring, shaping, guiding, bringing out every nuance of meaning and emotion—tapping a beat, whistling a tune, or conducting a symphony, the spirit of music is always there.

How Do They Do It?:
The Powerful Poems of Dorianne Laux and
B. H. Fairchild

Am I imagining, or is the word *powerful* applied to poetry less than it used to be? A quick sampling of the back covers of recent collections garnered many words of praise—*dazzling, erudite, tragi-comic, gorgeous, brilliant, tender, honest, original, formally accomplished, heartbreaking, wrenching, devastating, musical, mystical, thought-provoking, ironic, inventive, strange, sophisticated, serious, subtle, poignant, approachable, transrational, wise* . . .[215]—but, though *heart-breaking, wrenching,* and *devastating* come close to the sadder part of *powerful,* power seems not to be what blurbers celebrate these days.

In some ways, this is no surprise. Power has gotten a bad name. Much current English scholarship concerns abuse of it. To have it seems unfair; to give oneself up to someone else's seems servile, masochistic, primitive. Sophisticated readers are reluctant (or should be, they are told) to relinquish power by acknowledging authorial *authority.* The reader is the real creator. The author is dead; and good riddance to the fascist s.o.b.

Still, after reading poems by B. H. Fairchild and Dorianne Laux this semester, my MFA students were floored.

"Fairchild's work is just so . . . *powerful,*" one student said, as if he'd discovered a new superlative.

"Her work's *intense.* And really moving," another said of Laux. "How does she do it?"

---

215 Also *lyrical, well-made, heart-felt, cool, composed, unpredictable, risky, necessary, frightening, dark, spirited, accessible, painterly, elegiac, complex, sorrowing, exuberant, real, eloquent, fearless, compassionate, unflinching, resonant, subversive, deft, beautiful, sly, ambitious, urgent, truthful, elegant, non-sequential, bountiful, confrontational, funny, keen-sighted, sharp-edged, wry, gentle, wistful, radical, lucid, improvisational, articulate, smart, harrowing, astonishing, dangerous, post-avant, postmodern, meticulous, scholarly, technically masterful, transgressive, luminous, quiet, meditative, (unapologetically) cerebral, complex, defiant, ambiguous, open-ended, magical . . .*

By "it," the student meant *hit hard emotionally*—bring a lump to the throat, knot to the gut, tear to the eye. He meant what Emily Dickinson meant when she said that real poetry blew off the top of her head.

Both Fairchild and Laux affect my cranium that way. How *do* they do it? Fairchild's "Rave On" starts this way:

> Rumbling over caliche with a busted muffler,
> radio blasting Buddy Holly over Baptist wheat fields,
> Travis screaming out *Prepare ye the way of the Lord*
> at jackrabbits skittering beneath our headlights,
> the Messiah coming to Kansas in a flat-head Ford
> with bad plates, the whole high plains holding its breath,
> night is fast upon us, lo, in these the days of our youth . . .[216]

Technically, these lines are masterful. With their strong, mostly six-beat cadence, they gather momentum like the flat-head Ford they conjure, rolling on and on. Their rhythm proclaims loudly, "This is more than chat." The short *u*'s of *rumbling, busted, muffler*; the *b*'s of *busted, blasting, Buddy, Baptist*; the long *e*'s of *caliche, wheat, fields, screaming, ye*, all help to evoke a heightened, excited state. And all of this happens in the first three lines.

Yet, despite the sonic fireworks, this is Wordsworth's "real language of men."[217] The lines ring true to their subject—authentic and natural. *Caliche* evokes the harsh, barren land of the high plains as first seen by Spanish conquistadores. "Busted muffler" is the very phrase boys would use to describe the thing. *Prepare ye the way of the lord* evokes the religious flavor of 1950s Kansas, imparting a grandeur and gravitas to the poem.[218]

There's nothing stuffy, though, about the lines—nothing pious, self-righteous, or sermon-serious. There's room for humor here, from Travis screaming Bible verses at jackrabbits, to the friends "dragging Main Street shit-faced on 3.2 beer, / and banging on the whorehouse door in Garden City, / where the ancient madam laughed and turned us down / since we were only boys, and she knew our fathers."[219]

---

216 B. H. Fairchild, *Early Occult Memory Systems of the Lower Midwest* (New York: W.W. Norton & Company, 2003): 27–31.

217 William Wordsworth, Preface to *Lyrical Ballads* (Boston: Houghton Mifflin Company, 1962): 8.

218 Fairchild continues this use of religious language—"groweth" (line 27), "yea" (line 28), "belly of the whale" (line 45), "fainteth" (line 46), "sore afraid" (line 54), etc.

219 Fairchild, *Early Occult Memory Systems of the Lower Midwest*, 27.

The whole idea of the "Messiah come to Kansas in a flat-head Ford" is funny, yet also serious. The Ford would seem apocalyptic to the skittering jackrabbits. And the sound of "lo, in these the days of our youth," adding the religious *lo* to a Byronic allusion,[220] give this line a mix of comedy and grandeur. The line is humorously overblown, and seriously not.

Fairchild's poem maintains or exceeds this level of rhetorical intensity for 123 lines. That kind of length is another way to achieve power—if you avoid running out of gas.

Another means by which Fairchild powers his poem is good old-fashioned storytelling. His tale of teenage boys who risk death by rolling a car at high speed, hooked me and held on tight. Fairchild, whose writing shows a deep love of movies, can also write cinematically. His description of the Ford tumbling across the Kansas plains—the boys inside not even wearing seatbelts!—is as exciting as the same scene would be in a movie.

The boys roll the car, hoping this act of daring will change them into men. Here is another source of Fairchild's power: he dares to tackle "big" subjects and "heavy" themes. In "Rave On," these include 1. the nature of manhood, 2. coming to grips with the loss of youth and dreams, and 3. the search for meaning in, not just post-Darwinian existence, but human *life*.

In "Body and Soul,"[221] another powerhouse poem (which tells a great story of young Mickey Mantle used as a ringer in a baseball game), Fairchild explores manhood and the nature of genius, set against a backdrop of thwarted lives, demolished dreams, life-sapping jobs, and just soldiering on. He even dares to write a long poem, "Beauty,"[222] in which he explores—with the help of more great stories—that large, profound, and now unfashionable theme.

Although "Body and Soul" addresses, in a way that would please a narrative psychotherapist, the stories people tell to make sense of their lives, the poem contains no self-reflexive interrogation of the nature of *writer* and *narrative* in a post-post age, no fretting about the limits of communication, not one absurdist fairy tale or associative tour de force. There's not even hip-and-knowing irony. What there is in Fairchild's work, above all else, is wonderful writing.

---

220 "The days of our youth are the days of our glory," from "All for Love," by George Gordon, Lord Byron.

221 B. H. Fairchild, *The Art of the Lathe* (Farmington: Alice James Books, 1998): 35–38.

222 Ibid., 11–18.

> I survived. We all did. And then came the long surrender,
> the long, slow drifting down like young hawks riding on
> the purest, thinnest air, the very palm of God
> holding them aloft so close to something hidden there,
> and then the letting go, the fluttering descent, claws
> spread wide against the world, and we become, at last,
> our fathers . . .[223]

Lines like those give "Rave On" power because they're so well done—so apt and beautiful and true.

Truth—rare and dangerous as uranium—can be a huge power source. It certainly is in the work of Dorianne Laux—known for dealing frankly and clearly, in relatively short poems, with the very big subjects of sex and love.

In "Fast Gas," she uses deceptively simple diction to seduce us into the poem.

> Before the days of self service,
> when you never had to pump your own gas,
> I was the one who did it for you, the girl
> who stepped out at the sound of a bell
> with a blue rag in my hand, my hair pulled back
> in a straight, unlovely ponytail.[224]

This is the plain style at its best: natural and apparently artless. Yet scanning reveals a free-flowing, loosely iambic line of four to six beats. The smooth, caressing rhythm sets up a sexy story: the girl gets splashed with gas and, soaking wet, has to change clothes in a small bathroom without a lock. The language in this part of the poem keeps up its iambic caress, becoming more and more sexually charged as the speaker lists her wet body parts—"face, breasts, belly and legs," then peels off her wet clothes and scrubs her skin that "shimmered and ached, glowed / like rainbowed oil."

At any instant, someone could walk into the restroom and, porno-style, discover her. But no, the climax (so to speak) is delayed for weeks until she meets a man with "the kind of beauty / that asks to be noticed." The literal

---

223 Fairchild, *Early Occult Memory Systems of the Lower Midwest*, 30.
224 Dorianne Laux, *What We Carry* (Rochester: BOA Editions, 1994): 52–53.

gasoline is gone from her flesh, but the metaphorical explosive has lain in wait until he finds her:

> an ordinary woman who could rise
> in flame, all he would have to do
> is come close and touch me.[225]

The first of these three concluding lines is iambic pentameter, gentle and measured, but with a *rise* in pitch and excitement at the end. The penultimate line can be read as iambic tetrameter; however, following the strong caesura after *flame*, the words make an anapestic rush toward the last line. This can be scanned as one iamb, one trochee, and one spondee; but it moves more like two bacchic feet—"is COME CLOSE and TOUCH ME"— the rhythm mirroring an overpowering sexual impulse to touch deeply, and touch hard.

Laux uses similarly seductive metrics in "2 AM," which begins in medias res:

> When I came with you that first time
> on the floor of your office, the dirty carpet
> under my back, the heel of one foot
> propped on your shoulder, I went ahead
> and screamed, full-throated, as loud
> and as long as my body demanded . . .[226]

The accents here seem more intense than in "Fast Gas," at least partly because of what they describe. These are loosely iambic, mainly four beat lines, but still very much plain speech: direct, honest, and urgent. By the end, though, this sexually explicit poem has taken on some of the religious sensibility that helps to power "Rave On."

> And when you finally spoke, you didn't
> lift your head, but simply moaned the word *god*,
> on an exhalation of breath—I knew then

---

225 Laux, *What We Carry.*
226 Ibid., 62–63.

I must be merciful, benevolent,
impossibly kind.[227]

The male seems literally to worship the female speaker: a pagan goddess who aspires toward at least some Christ-like virtues. The penultimate line, with its Latinate, Christian vocabulary, is pure iambic pentameter. Then the last line hits us with five accents—at least four strong ones—in just five syllables. Though it lacks a concrete image, it hits hard rhythmically and emotionally.

Imagery is another source of Laux's power. Her lines are full of striking pictures, from the gas "arcing out of the hole / in a bright gold wave,"[228] to the spent lover, his body seeming ". . . defeated, owned, having taken on / the aspect of a slave in shackles, the wrists / loosely bound . . ."[229]

Laux's metaphors can be amazing—the gas-soaked girl, for instance, ready to explode in flames. Yet perhaps the greatest source of her poems' power is her voice: vulnerable, tender, insightful, warm, compassionate, lusty with no snickering or self-absorption, no boasting, but also no mocking of the sexual needs and strivings of the flesh. The first time I read "2 AM," I felt stripped naked, amazed that someone—a woman, no less—could speak so truthfully about male sexual vulnerability.[230]

Laux's poems about sexual love are consistently stunning. Even when her speaker is awkward and self-conscious, she records her experience honestly and un-self-consciously. In a culture that continues to struggle with sexuality, Laux's approach seems absolutely right—not prim or pious, not lewd or depraved, not clinical, ironic, joking, detached, or protesting too much—just thoroughly human, humane, and psychologically healthy. The power of that health is hard to overstate.

To the dozen power sources already stated—

1. Effective technique
2. Authenticity
3. Religious/spiritual overtones (without piety or cant)
4. Seriousness (with room for humor)

---

227 Ibid.
228 Ibid., 52.
229 Ibid., 62.
230 She does the same for females in "The Lovers," Ibid., 64–65.

5. Good stories, dramatically told
6. Cinematic action-writing
7. Willingness to tackle "big"/"heavy" themes
8. Explosive metaphors and imagery
9. Truth-telling/insight
10. Compassion
11. Vulnerability
12. Healthy sexuality

—we should add a thirteenth: the much-derided *Accessibility*. Both Fairchild and Laux write poetry that is available to any literate person, with or without an advanced degree, or any degree at all.

Their poetry is not "experimental" in the avant-garde sense. Both poets seem unconcerned with postmodern literary theory or attitudes.[231] Showing no interest in promulgating new ways of reading, or radically altering the way in which English is used, they seem to be trying their best to speak directly and truthfully to the reader, with no trickery or obfuscation. Neither do their most powerful poems rely on fashionable irony or self-reflexive mugging to an in-crowd audience. They use humor, but not to condescend or mock. They do not self-aggrandize, or write for the happy few. Fairchild and Laux honor ordinary lives.

It's one thing, though, to list some power sources, and even to explain how they work. It's quite another to explain where such power ultimately comes from—let alone how to get it into poems.

Explicators love to show poets using sound to mirror sense. Yet no real poet thinks, "I want to dramatize the sexual impulse to touch deeply and touch hard. I know! I'll use two Bacchic feet!" Skilled poets manipulate sound consciously, but also instinctively. When the instinct is good, we say the poet has "a good ear."

So how do you get one of those? And how does one write *authentically*? Does any serious poet, except perhaps the post-post-post variety, try to write *in*authentically?

Practice makes more adept, it's true. You can't play Beethoven's piano concertos or write "The Love Song of J. Alfred Prufrock" without a lot of practice. But practice is not enough. Talent—whatever that is—is not enough. Practice plus talent is not enough. Each and every power source

---

231 This does not mean that these avant-garde approaches can't produce powerful poetry, only that they do not factor into the work under discussion here.

in our baker's dozen is an outward manifestation of inner qualities—of *personality*.

T. S. Eliot notwithstanding,[232] writers *must* create from their personalities. They may, in Walt Whitman's words, "contain multitudes"; but they contain them within a single self. As Whitman stated in his diary, "Understand that you cannot keep out of your writing the indication of the evil or shallowness that you entertain in yourself . . . [Nor is there any] trick or cunning, no art or recipe, by which you can have in your writing what you do not possess in yourself."[233]

Without an emotionally powerful personality, no one can write powerful poems.

How do poets gain emotional power? How can they get it into poems?

Over years of doing psychotherapy with artists, I've found that, to make powerful art, the artist must:

1. Sincerely want to make it
If, like some contemporary poets, you distrust strong emotions, or for any number of reasons are not interested in writing poems that elicit them, you probably won't.

2. Approve of expressing personal power and powerful emotions
Many people in our culture are embarrassed by strong emotion, and fear losing control. For many years, one of our most common adjectives of approbation has been *cool*. How can we expect to write powerful poems if our personal ideal is to be always calm, unruffled, in control?

Another much-admired virtue, at least in educated circles, is to be non-judgmental. Yeats's famous lines, "The best lack all conviction, while the worst / Are full of passionate intensity,"[234] have been absorbed into the self-image of many intellectuals, who view passionate intensity with distrust and distaste. But any strong emotion requires a strong judgment. It's hard to generate much power from a seat on the fence.

Writers who want to evoke powerful emotions must feel good about having and expressing them. They must search out, rather than—as most

---

232 "Poetry is not the expression of personality but an escape from personality," Eliot, "Tradition and the Individual Talent," in *The Sacred Wood*.

233 Bliss Perry, *Walt Whitman: His Life and Work* (Boston: Houghton Mifflin and Company, 1906): 72.

234 William Butler Yeats, "The Second Coming," in *Selected Poems and Two Plays of William Butler Yeats* (New York: Collier Books, 1962): 91.

people do—avoid subjects that brings out those emotions. Then they must address those subjects fearlessly.

3. Lower psychological defenses

The effectiveness of and necessity for psychological defense mechanisms is well-documented. Their result, however, is to distance people from their most powerful impulses.

Rebuked unfairly by her boss, A's deepest desire may be to kill him painfully. With the aid of defense mechanisms, the dangerous energy of that response may be re-channeled into understanding (pardoning, or feeling superior to the boss), resolving to work harder and earn the boss's approval, or even punishing herself for the rebuke.

If Fairchild's grief at the loss of youth had been modified by a defense mechanism—telling himself, "Ah well, all things must change," or "Think of the trouble I had as a kid. I'm glad to be out of there"—"Rave On" could have been one long platitude. If Laux had defended against her knowledge of the male lover's helplessness and the female's power—"I shouldn't be so presumptuous, so egotistical, so intemperate. I need to moderate my feelings, my response . . ."—"2 AM" might have become "A Nice Woman Has Sex and Feels Uneasy Afterward."

To write a powerful poem, the poet's full instinctual energy must be available.

4. Cast off modesty and deference

I'm not advising that poets do this in their lives. But if you want to write powerfully, you must, while you are writing, don the Mantle of Power—even if you choose to disguise the fact. You must command, "Call me Ishmael," not suggest, "If it's not too much trouble, and you agree, you might consider calling me Ishmael." The universe, of which you are a part, speaks through you!

Even if it doesn't, it helps to write as if it does. You can always revise . . .

5. Be open to all aspects of power

A poet may write a powerful poem out of one powerful emotion. To write consistently powerful work, it helps to be open to them all. Yet this openness requires risk.

While training as a psychotherapist, I learned that when our teachers asked us to "get in touch" with our emotions, they meant the sad ones.

Overly happy emotions—elation, high spirits, exultation—were seen as
shallow and/or unseemly. Angry emotions—especially when linked with
a drive to kick someone's behind—might lead to dismissal from the program. Anger was viewed not as a primary emotion, but a primitive defense
against sadness. When linked to physical power, it was very bad indeed.
Ferocity, however well-controlled, was not welcomed on either side of the
therapy divide.

Similar attitudes are not uncommon among readers of contemporary
poetry. If a male poet were to celebrate the power—physical or otherwise—of men in sex, then announce that he had to be "merciful, benevolent / impossibly kind," he might well be called a pig, or worse. "How
condescending!" "What—a little kindness would kill you?"

So be it. To make powerful art, one must also:

6. Be willing to be harshly criticized

You may avoid criticism by celebrating—moderately—things you're sure
that your audience likes, and satirizing things of which you're sure it dis-
approves. Or you may write with such thorough irony that it's clear you've
seen the fatuousness of all human life, and scorn everything. You can refuse to take a stand; or you can write in such an "indeterminate" way that
you could stand for anything.

In none of those cases are you likely to write powerful poems.

It's not easy to stand psychologically naked, undefended and unrepen-
tant, before an audience of intellectuals, many of whom get more pleasure
out of criticizing than admiring. And make no mistake: if you stalk big
emotional game, you'll often come back skunked. When you fail, you may
fail big. And unlike in "experimental" work, where success can be hard to
tell from failure, and the poet can always blame the audience, your failure
will be obvious, and on display.

To write powerful poems, poets must care more about the truth as
they see it, than how good they look telling it, or how others will react. A
writer who is clearly and emotionally present in his/her work makes an
easy target for ridicule, like Caruso in a clown suit. Critic William Logan,
to whom ridicule comes easy, dumped a truckload on *Early Occult Memory Systems of the Lower Midwest*[235]—the same book that knocked me and
my students out.

---

235 William Logan, "The real language of men," in *The New Criterion* (December 2002): 6–12.

Lift your head above a crowd, and—count on it—someone will try to knock it off. That is one price of power.

I take as axiomatic that, since strong emotions were vital to our evolutionary survival, everyone has them to some degree, and therefore, has the potential to write powerful poems. To increase that emotional power, a writer must exercise it.

I don't mean get in a screaming session with the spouse. I mean become more aware of emotions as they occur. Become familiar and at ease with your emotional landscape. Dare to go anywhere inside your mind. Learn when you're suppressing emotion, and what emotion is suppressed.

Don't settle for surface emotions; those spawn clichés. Couples don't fight over taking out the trash; deep issues are always in play. Power, like *architeuthis*, lives in the depths. To write powerfully, you need to go down there, even if you fear what you find.

Be forewarned: Civilized life goes more smoothly when emotions are suppressed. Becoming more aware of yours may bring you into conflict with yourself and others. It may lead to radical changes in your life. That's why so many people stay emotionally shut down.

Power, in poems or out, is not for the faint of heart. Like jumping across a chasm, power requires commitment. No looking down mid-flight. No stopping halfway and turning back. Power is not for those easily dissuaded by what other people think. It requires someone strong enough to take a stand, then take the flak that comes flying.

Literary theorists like to speak about unstable narrators, fluid personalities, "the slippery I." But real human personalities are remarkably stable over time. Psychotherapy would be a breeze if the psyche reinvented itself one tenth as easily as some theorists seem to think it can. "A less defined consciousness, speaking without need of or reference to a particular situation"[236] may be a useful literary device, but it is pure artifice. It may allow for interesting effects. But emotional power requires at least one well-defined consciousness faced with a particular situation in which something major is at stake.

Poetry is written by real people whose consciousness is well-defined, whether they know it or not. Words communicate, whether the author believes in communication, or does not. I read in hopes of receiving mean-

---

236 Matthew Zapruder, "Show Your Work," www.poetryfoundation.org/archive/print.html?id=186047 (March 2009).

ingful communication. If the communication is, "I'm interested in dis-
tancing, distracting, obscuring, and erecting barriers between you and me,"
I'm not inclined to listen long—unless I'm doing therapy. For a large fee.

Oscar Wilde quipped, "All bad poetry springs from genuine feeling."[237]
But all genuine feeling does not lead to bad poetry. One of the great
strengths of Fairchild's and Laux's work is that it feels genuine. Whitman
says that writers can't hide who they are. Fairchild and Laux don't apparently need to.

Fairchild's poem "Body and Soul" ends with these lines:

> When I see my friend's father staring hard into the bottomless
> well of home plate as Mantle's fifth homer heads toward Arkansas,
> I know that this man with the half-orphaned children and
> worthless Dodge has also encountered for his first and possibly
> only time the vast gap between talent and genius, has seen
> as few have in the harsh light of an Oklahoma Sunday, the blonde
> and blue-eyed bringer of truth, who will not easily be forgiven.[238]

The first time I read this, tears jumped into my eyes. I recommended the
poem to my sister who, like most people, reads almost no poetry. She cried
at the end, too. Then one of my students—a retired bank executive—read
the poem aloud as part of an assignment, and—in front of the whole class
of embarrassed 20-somethings—began to weep.[239]

Were these tears because the three of us love baseball? Because we miss
the days of Mickey Mantle? Because we didn't grow up to be him? Because
we're too old to pretend we have genius, can't forgive those who spotlight
our lack, and weep to see this and other truths about our lives? Does Fairchild, and Laux as well, practice some dark emotional art?

Who knows? Part of art's power is that it rises, finally, out of the mystery of human consciousness.

But is powerful art still a good thing? Is it relevant in a jaded, disillusioned postmodern world? Or is it a sham/manipulation/power-grab—a
wiener trying to seem a Frankfurter by donning a Hitler moustache?

---

237 Oscar Wilde, "The Critic as Artist," in *The Complete Works of Oscar Wilde*, Vol. 4, ed. Jo-
sephine M. Guy (London: Oxford University Press): 195.

238 Fairchild, *The Art of the Lathe*, 38.

239 If your own tears aren't already staining the page, please be aware that this passage comes
after a masterfully written 110-line poem in which the reader learns exactly how much was at
stake in a long-ago baseball game lost to the fifteen-year-old Mantle.

When it's easier, safer, cooler, hipper, and more fun to pump irony, do associational gymnastics, glide over high experimental hurdles to the applause of the crowd (what's left of it), why concern ourselves with dangerous and atavistic emotions?

I do it because these emotions help me to slit the straitjacket of civilized life—to feel more deeply, and live more fully in the process. I do it because Ezra Pound—whose war-cry was "Make it new"—was right to say, "Only emotion endures."[240]

In most areas of human life, the new quickly becomes old. But powerful emotion, artfully expressed, doesn't age. Hector's sadness and Achilles's anger still ring true—fresh, exciting, deeply human—after many centuries. Only emotion endures because, in art, only emotion has the power to stay new.

---

240 Ezra Pound, "A Retrospect," in *Pavannes and Divagations* (New York: Knopf, 1918).

When Goodness Is Not a Virtue:
Morality, Psychology, and Poetry

America is swimming in good poetry. More and more poets pump out more and more poems with good imagery, effective rhythms, skillful line breaks, no obvious clichés. More and more magazines, presses, and websites publish this poetry. Yet the news is not, as my young male students like to say, "all good."

Much of this poetry is well-made but tame—lacking what Freud called "Id" energy: the violent, selfish, cruel, angry, aggressive, dangerous excesses that make *Homo sapiens* fully human, and art come alive. Many a prestigious magazine offers a showroom full of neutered lap dogs, not a wolf in sight.

Much contemporary poetry today, whether mainstream or avant-garde, is, in Tony Hoagland's words, "constrained by . . . the unstated wish to be admired (if not admired, liked; if not liked, sympathized with)."[241] But how many of us not-so-virtuous readers want to watch a poet advertise his or her admirability? The absolutely good narrator of a poem is likely to be boring and a liar. Since, by definition, he or she conforms entirely to a pre-packaged value system, the chance of moral surprise is slim-to-none. If the value system comes from humanistic psychotherapy, the problem becomes, as we will see, acute.

Consider *The Odyssey*. Odysseus not only kills all of Penelope's suitors on his return; he kills twelve of her maids for consorting with them. First he makes them clean his halls of the killed suitors' blood; then he hangs them. After that, Melanthius, a goatherd who had mocked and assaulted the disguised Odysseus, has his nose and ears cut off, his hands and feet severed, his genitals fed to dogs. Of course, Odysseus was not constrained

---

241 Tony Hoagland, "Negative Capability: How To Talk Mean and Influence People," in *Real Sofistikashun*, 197.

by humanistic values, much less by political correctness—PC[242]—which does to the psyche, and Art, more or less what Odysseus did to Melanthius.

So why the current onslaught of gelded goodness in poetry?

Weakness in the market place. Unlike prose fiction—much of which is published in hope of big sales, and in which there is usually at least one Id-driven antagonist—even the most accessible poetry does not have or hope for a mass audience, and therefore does not need to appeal to one. Art intended for big sales cannot be dull; and Art that lacks Id energy almost always is. Poetry, then, can afford unmitigated goodness; prose fiction cannot.

The good student syndrome. Every teacher wants good students; no teacher wants trouble. It's no surprise that in the creative writing classroom—the main launching pad for poetry careers—those who please the teacher and don't make trouble get on best.

Most troublesome students wear their pathology, not just on their sleeve, but all over their wardrobe. They are more likely to need meds than to be the geniuses they think they are. But the talented nonconformist who does not please—the rebel with a just cause and something original, and maybe threatening, to say—may have a hard time with the teacher, and a harder time with fellow students. Consequently, there are strong incentives not to be such a student, and if you are one, to go away.

Thou shalt not offend. Like politicians, students in writing workshops are conditioned not to rock the moral boat. Every veteran of workshops has seen classes hijacked by the moral and/or political beliefs of one or more participants.[243] Group muggings of offenders have occurred, and are not easily forgotten. As a result, poems and poets from the workshop culture tend to be "socially responsible" and highly PC. Real-life Humbert Humbert, or their chroniclers, are not welcome in that world. There must be no racists, sexists, homophobes, highwaymen. No Eliot, Pound, Larkin, or Villon.

Careerism. In the days when almost no one made a living at it, the world of poetry harbored many non-conformists. Nowadays, when successful Po-Bizzers operate a lot like other businesspeople—networking,

---

242 Secular humanism gave rise to humanistic psychology, which produced humanistic psychotherapy, which promulgated and popularized the attitudes and vision which came to be called—first humorously, then seriously, then both—politically correct, or PC, the politics referred to being the left-wing, progressive kind.

243 The situation is worst when the participant is the professor.

trading favors, managing their images—the true original may not fare well. As the rewards for poetry have grown, many poets have become at least as interested in career development as poem development.

Like attracts like. Besides such qualities as love of language and literature, people drawn to poetry tend to share—with each other, their teachers, and the poetry powers-that-be—similar worldviews, aspirations, politics, and even temperaments. Small wonder if their work is morally similar.

Fashion-consciousness. Poets of today—especially those from high-prestige MFA programs—know very well what is hip and what is square, at least in their part of the poetry world. If they don't know it going *into* their programs, they know it coming out. And, truth be told, if they don't know it going in, they are a lot less likely to *get* in.

Artistic timidity. Poets trained to rigorous standards by demanding teachers may become accomplished mimics who fear criticism more than they love exploration. They don't know how to "fool around"—an activity central to creativity and innovation. For them, the practice of poetry becomes more about avoiding censure than taking the kind of risks that lead to artistic breakthroughs and compelling Art.

I hear you saying . . . Virtually all Americans well-educated in the Liberal Arts have internalized the values of humanistic psychotherapy. These include the so-called "curative factors" respect, empathy, self-disclosure, caring, warmth, and hope. Adherents to these values are sensitive to others' feelings, and therefore, averse to competition, since winning means that someone else must lose. They distrust "controlling" people, and "rugged individualists," especially white, heterosexual males. Left-leaning in their politics, they tend to value certain kinds of self-revelation as prima facie evidence of moral and artistic merit, to crave consensus, and to fear appearing "judgmental" (except, perhaps, when labeling others *judgmental*). They abominate physical fighting, and have a near-religious faith in the verbal kind: a sense that any disagreement can be "talked out."

Naturally enough, in a value system so closely linked with psychotherapy, there is a strong preference for talk, thought, and rumination over decisive (and most likely, un-nuanced) action. Monty Python satirizes this humanistic/intellectual preference when a plane hijacker bursts into the cockpit, yells "Don't anyone move," then proceeds to quibble and qualify his statement. "I don't want to be dogmatic. Of course your hearts have to beat . . ." and on and on.

Yeats's famous words, "The best lack all conviction . . .," seem to have been embraced with pride by poets who abjure meaning, coherence, and any notion of "absolute" reality. Writers and readers alike fear to be found guilty of the fascism of saying X means *this* (and not *that*), or of trying to guide the reader to think or feel in a particular way.

Even the notion of *beauty* may be rejected as subjective, culture-bound, hurtful to the not-beautiful, and ultimately coercive, totalitarian, and bourgeois. The feeling seems to be that, if we and what we make can't all be beautiful, then beauty is elitist and immoral. It should not, and therefore *does* not, exist.

Although the psychotherapeutic systems of Freud and Jung emphasize the darker side of the human personality—Freud's "Id," and Jung's "Shadow"—humanistic psychotherapy emphasizes compassionate, altruistic, egalitarian impulses. Poems that share these values tend to lack the Id energy that Freud saw as powering artistic expression. They go light on the "Shadow," integration of which Jung saw as essential for healthy human beings. They are, it turns out, intensely PC.

Stressing civility, compassion, and general goodness, PC poets can't tap the power that comes from facing and embracing the dark side. Cut off from important parts of themselves, they can't write with the full force of the human personality. In Freudian terms, they've lost the power of their instinctive drives, and limited their own access to their unconscious minds, where the best art is born.

The work of Sylvia Plath shows dramatically the difference between a mediocre "good" poet, and a great "bad" one. Plath's early poems are earnest, serious, and try very hard. Many poets would be thrilled to write this well; but if poems such as the early "November Graveyard"[244] (text available on the Internet) were all we had, Plath would likely be a footnote today.

Her poem begins with an anthropomorphized image of trees as misers hoarding leaves, refusing to sorrow for the coming winter, or to display any ennobling magic by turning into dryads. The grass is "dour" and "hard-hearted," however deeply the human mind yearns for something more lush and imaginative.

There is, the second stanza lets us know, nothing romantic about this graveyard. There is only "honest rot," countering the human tendency to

244 Sylvia Plath, "November Graveyard" in *The Collected Poems*, ed. Ted Hughes (New York: Harper Perennial, 1992): 56.

fantasize about an afterlife or, at least, something nobler than decomposition.

The final stanza wraps things up by restating the poet's belief that the supernatural is a product of human minds starved for meaning and unwilling to confront life's emptiness. So there!

The verbal energy and bleak vision of Plath's later poems are here: ". . . When one stark skeleton / Bulks real, all saints' tongues fall quiet:" But the imagery leans heavily on pathetic fallacy. It strains, coming at readers from so many directions that it seems to blur. The language feels self-consciously poetic—heavy alliteration and internal rhyme, a struggle every line to coin a ringing phrase. The poem shows all the signs of an *A* student striving to emulate her Masters, and win their praise. In other pre-1960 poems, Plath seems eager to display her knowledge, and to sound the way she seems to think a real (i.e., male) poet should.[245] Her poems echo with the sounds of Eliot, Thomas, and Ted Hughes. Even her subjects invite praise. *Real poets write poems about graveyards, so here's mine.*

Plath's early poems have their virtues, but despite attempts at pyrotechnics, they don't transfix the reader with a vision and a voice that is startling, unique, and unmistakable. For all their surface *sturm und drang,* they could have been written by any number of promising poets of the time. Plath's message in "November Graveyard"—that despite the human wish for transcendence, death is only death—might have scandalized a pilgrim at the first Thanksgiving; in 1956, it was not news.

Plath's intellect is fully engaged in her early poems; her psyche is not. With the perceptiveness of hindsight, we can feel her wild Id energy straining to break through; but it stays in check. Nothing shocking emerges—nothing that would have made people in her literary circle cringe. The essential Sylvia isn't there.

She diagnosed this problem herself, and wrote of it in July 1960, just four years after "November Graveyard," and barely two from the creative outburst that made her reputation, and chronicled the state of mind that led to her suicide. In her poem "Stillborn"[246] (text available on the Internet), she laments that her poems "do not live."

Her diagnosis is right. For all her hard work and earnest striving, Plath's early poems lack the Id energy that brings art to life. Instead, "They sit so

---

245 Her poem "Sow," for instance, seems as bloated as its subject, which is simply, "Wow, that's a big pig."

246 Plath, *The Collected Poems,* 142.

nicely in the pickling fluid"—too proper, too scrupulously well-made, too eager to please. Pure goodness does not make a whole person, nor does it make a living poem. Her dead poems "stupidly stare, and do not speak of her"—i.e., the *real* her.

Ironically, Plath's poem about dead poems is much more alive than "November Graveyard." Plain and direct, the language doesn't strain, yet packs a punch. The central images of stillbirth are vividly realized, genuinely disturbing. The writer is no student trying to imitate a poet. The real Sylvia, if not fully arrived, is on her way.

Plath the person might have done better to hold her Id energy at bay. If she had, she might be alive—if less famous—today. But mental illness overwhelmed the good girl, rushing out in her last two years with the ferocity that has made Plath a name even non-poets recognize.

In her volcanic last poems—"Lady Lazarus," "The Applicant," "Daddy," etc.—the good girl is gone, gone, gone. Rage, venom, forbidden urges, Medean grief, violence, and spite erupt in a voice that is hers alone.

Those three poems contain vivid, glamorous images of suicide, homicide, patricide, Nazis, masochism, father-hate, and incestuous love. Plath mocks, satirizes, and indicts the "good" wife, the "good" woman, God, the handicapped, and the institution of marriage. She makes flippant references to Jews and the Holocaust. She uses ethnic slurs. She throws unwholesome images in our face, from bad breath and striptease to devil-worship. She revels in "bad taste," indulging in humor of the darkest kind, as when she equates worms eating the dead to "sticky pearls." These poems would have been shocking for a man to have written in 1962. For a woman, they were astonishing. Her poems, obsessed with Eros and Thanatos, rise directly out of her unconscious: horrifying, and intensely original and alive.

Plath is, of course, an extreme case. To write living poems, poets don't have to be mentally ill; they don't have to die so that their poems can live. They can't afford, though, to be deferential, meek, or politically correct in their poetry. They can't go in fear of "darker" urges, or write purely out of the conscious mind.

Yet, browsing through new publications, I see more "good" poetry than any other kind. It's not that the poets can't write, so much as that they're afraid to say something that might shock someone—possibly themselves. Their failure is not of craft, but of courage. Smothered under puffy pillows of acceptability, Imagination can't breathe, or even lift its head.

Here are some notes I've made while reading recent books of poems.

1. *Very careful work. Low-key, restrained, withholding, controlled. No bad lines here. No really good ones.*
2. *These poems equivocate. They don't come down hard anywhere. Tough to pin them down enough to evaluate. Tough to like.*
3. *Linguistically obscure, evasive, coy about plot/emotion/attitude. Once deciphered, they prove banal.*
4. *The author speaks of socially conscious subjects—homelessness, minorities, the underprivileged, other cultures—in predictable ways. How much wiser are the Gorgonzola tribe than we!*
5. *Creative Writing maxims on display. Verbs are REALLY active. Nouns are REALLY strange. Almost nothing a real person would say. Poems work so hard to be lyrical, they become precious, mannered, false. Exhausting to get through even one.*
6. *Look at me! Look how much I know! Pedantry instead of passion.*
7. *This poet sits pretty on a well-trained horse, but won't go near a hot, wild one. Even the poem about stinks seems fastidious. "I like to talk about icky things, but I don't want to sound icky. Don't forget I'm educated, sensitive, lyrical, refined."*
8. *Well-written, but static, lacking fire. Nothing shouts "Wake up!" Nothing astonishes.*
9. *A virtue show-off. High wimp-quotient here. Careful steps, versus impetuous leaps. Sid Sawyer, not Tom.*
10. *Poems are wry, knowing, ironic, veiled, fashionably jaded and satirically surreal. They flaunt all the values of the hip young literati, and take no moral or stylistic risks at all.*

I'm not suggesting that a first-rate writer has to be a rogue or sociopath. But it helps if he or she can think—and feel—like one.

Dylan Thomas's "Lament" mixes passionate, instinctual Id energy with a sense of humor. The poem paints goodness in a very bad light; but even if it did not, the sound of the poem—its rhythm, its fiery masculinity—reveals a verbal warrior in his prime, a slugger knocking it out of the literary park. No one who sounds like Dylan T. can be PC.

Tony Hoagland, who laments contemporary poets' avoidance of "subject matter that cannot be handled without contamination of the handler,"[247] has taken flack for his own poems that handle—and in his critics' eyes, seem to condone, or even advocate—racism and violence. Edward Field, Russell Edson, and Stephen Dobyns are all known for poems examining and celebrating Id energy. Frank O'Hara's well-known "Ave Maria," with its celebration of what would today be called child molestation, is rebellious, libidinous, high-spirited, and positively scandalous. But as Plath shows so convincingly, Id energy is not merely a male preoccupation, not a "testosterone thing."

Lucia Perillo's "The Crows Start Demanding Royalties" celebrates the pure delinquent cussedness of crows.

> The Crows Start Demanding Royalties
>
> Of all the birds, they are the ones
> who mind their being armless most:
> witness how, when they walk, their heads jerk
> back and forth like rifle bolts.
> How they heave their shoulders into each stride
> as if they hoped that by some chance
> new bones there would come popping out
> with a boxing glove on the end of each.
>
> Little Elvises, the hairdo slicked
> with too much grease, they convene on my lawn
> to strategize for their class-action suit.
> Flight they would trade in a New York minute
> for a black muscle car and a fist on the shift
> at any stale green light. But here in my yard
>
> by the Jack-in-the-Box Dumpster
> they can only fossick in the grass for remnants
>
> of the world's stale buns. And this
> despite all the crow poems that have been written
> because men like to see themselves as crows
> (the head-jerk performed in the rearview mirror,

---

247 Hoagland, "Negative Capability: How To Talk Mean and Influence People," in *Real Sofistikashun*, 197.

the dark brow commanding the rainy weather).
So I think I know how they must feel:
ripped off, shook down, taken to the cleaners.
What they'd like to do now is smash a phone against a wall.
But they can't, so each one flies to a bare branch and screams.[248]

Not only is the voice in this poem lively and compelling, Perillo captures the way crows—at least to humans—seem to be. Rifle bolts, boxing gloves, fists, muscle cars—the poem is full of aggressive imagery. The crows are portrayed as surly, hostile, enraged.

But this poem is about more than crows. Stanza three equates crows to men—not only in the poet's mind, but in the men's. Men are as obnoxious as crows, and glad to be so. But though the poem pokes fun at such men, its energy and brio celebrate them, too.

Stanza three reveals how the poet has gained such insight into crows and men. She knows "how they must feel." The speaker, too, feels surly, hostile, and enraged. The crows are mad, mean, and want to hurt people and things. The speaker does too. But she can't. So, like the crows, she flies to a bare branch (or book, or podium), and screams.

She also entertains. Just like people, poems with strong Id energy tend to be full of the qualities that make life and art not only meaningful, but exciting and even fun. Foremost among these are wit, passion, and impropriety.[249]

Wit. The importance to poetry of wit—meaning *quickness of perception, ingenuity, keen intelligence*—is self-evident. A poet who lacks this kind of wit will evince a low quality of thought.

Wit meaning *humor* can be important too. People who lack a sense of humor may, on first meeting, seem "nice"—even exceptionally so; but frequently, they pall. Nothing about them strikes sparks. Nothing seems fun. The imaginative leaps and unexpected connections characteristic of a first-rate mind may be absent. The sense of common humanity and the general uplift that laughter can provide are absent in the humorless person's conversation and poems.

---

248 Lucia Perillo, "The Crows Start Demanding Royalties," in *Luck is Luck* (New York: Random House, 2005): 10.

249 I have lifted the following three sections from "The Pleasure of Their Company: Voice and Poetry."

Passion. Passionate writing makes the reader come to grips with strong emotion. This is risky in a culture embarrassed by emotion, and even riskier when judgments about poems are made by critics and theorists who cultivate what they think is scientific detachment and objectivity.

To admit passion into poetry, as to admit love into one's life, is to risk being judged excessive, undiscriminating, jejune, ridiculous—especially if that passion is high-spirited and celebratory. To avoid such judgments, some poets cultivate understatement, obliqueness, and dour depressiveness.[250] They proceed by indirection, fearing to call a spade a spade and be told, "Idiot, that is a club."

How dreary, though, to speak with someone who lacks passion.[251] Like humorless people, the passionless may seem agreeable at first. But how "connect" with someone who is barely there? Eventually, we stop trying.

Impropriety in poetry is not the polar opposite of goodness, but the two are linked. Standards of propriety help to keep unpleasant, upsetting, dangerous realities out of mind. Politeness, which means suppressing what could make others uncomfortable, rules out much humor and most passion.

Employed for its own sake, impropriety is almost as uninteresting as strict propriety. However, since many truths are improper, indecorous, uncomfortable, and not PC, a person who avoids impropriety must avoid truth. The proper person, like the humorless and the passionless, will be dull. To escape controversy, such a person must censor imagination (who can tell where it will lead?), avoid penetrating insights (always potentially shocking), and keep excitement controlled (lest all hell break loose). Such a poet may create pretty pictures and artfully disguised homilies, but will be hard-pressed to make compelling art.

As a writer and a reader, I want poems that come at me like a fascinating person—lively, passionate, unlike anyone I've met before, with at least a touch of wildness and danger. I want unpredictable poems that might say *anything*.

I want poems with allegiance to the idiosyncratic, time-limited, non-dogmatic, possibly ignoble truth of experience—not poems concerned with how the poet is perceived. I want poems that excite, impas-

---

250 Poets whose work is subdued and depressive seem to get more respect than the high-spirited—due, apparently, to the belief that, if you're depressed, you must see the world accurately.
251 Sad to say, poets who are themselves passionate people not infrequently hold back that passion in their poems.

sion, amaze, electrify—poems with rough edges that cut—poems fully, proudly, defiantly human, and therefore not unequivocally and fashionably *good*. That kind of work first drew me to poetry; and it keeps me here. In a world that is increasingly encumbered and constrained, I want poems that exalt and embody life, wildness, freedom, and the totality of human experience—yang and yin, plus and minus, good and bad.

Anything less wastes all of our time.

The Quick and the Dead:
An Energy Crisis in Poetry

These poems do not live; it's a sad diagnosis.
—Sylvia Plath, "Stillborn"

Every semester, I send my poetry students to the library to browse through literary magazines. Their response is always more or less the same. The poems they find impress them as "intelligent," "knowledgeable," and "well-written"; yet too many strike them as "dull," "kind of dead," and "not something I'd really *want* to read."

Sad to say, I often feel the same way.

Charles Olson wrote, in 1950, "A poem is energy transferred from where the poet got it (he will have some several causations), by way of the poem itself, all the way over to the reader."[252] This energy can be imagined as a *charge* in the poet's brain, first transformed into a poem, then re-transformed, in the reader's brain, back to a charge. Just as strenuous exercise is incompatible with depression, high energy is incompatible with dullness. Both writer and reader experience poetic energy as a surge of interest and excitement—a palpable sense of life.

Energy may seem a questionable poetic virtue, linked with stocking-capped "performance" poets who punctuate shouted words with hip-hop gestures and gang signs. Like *duende*, energy is hard to define and quantify, much less to teach. Still, for poetry to be "the best words in the best order," those words and that order must have plenty of energy. Without it, words not only can't soar; they won't get off the ground.

Here are some forms poetic energy can take.

---

252 Charles Olson, "Projective Verse," in *Twentieth Century American Poetics*, ed. Dana Gioia, David Mason, and Meg Schoerke (New York: McGraw-Hill, 2004): 174.

1. Lexical energy

A good poet, by definition, uses words in interesting ways. Yet poets such
as Albert Goldbarth and Barbara Hamby demonstrate how interesting
words can, by themselves pump energy into poems.

Barbara Hamby's "My Translation" begins:

> I am translating the world into mockingbird, into blue jay,
> into cat-bombing avian obbligato, because I want
> more noise, more bells, more senseless tintinnabulation,
> more crow, thunder, squawk, more bird song,
> more Beethoven, more philharmonic mash notes to the gods . . .[253]

Albert Goldbarth's *"Ancestored-Back* Is the Overpresiding Spirit of This
Poem" is similarly full of energetic words.

> If only somebody would drill with a finger-long rig down
> into my skull, and saw a tiny circle out of its bone,
> so pools of acid antsiness and angst can steam away;
> so all of the great in-gnarling, all of the bunched up
> broodiness can breathe; and so at least the day's
> accumulated ephemera, its fenderbender squabbles,
> its parade of petty heartache can evaporate in writhes
> of sour mist . . .[254]

A word's interest can rise out of its meaning, history, etymology, strangeness, or sound. Whatever the source, a poem full of interesting words has
a head start when it comes to energy.

2. Syntactic energy

Some poems lie on the page as if they've been chloroformed. Others,
through the sheer muscularity of their sentence structure, kick up their
heels and run.

---

253 Barbara Hamby, "My Translation," in *Babel* (Pittsburgh: University of Pittsburgh Press, 2004): 3.
254 Albert Goldbarth, *"Ancestored-Back* Is the Overpresiding Spirit of This Poem," in *Contemporary American Poetry*, 8th ed., ed. A. Poulin, Jr. and Michael Waters (Boston: Houghton
Mifflin Company, 2006): 164.

> I saw the best minds of my generation destroyed by madness, starving
>   hysterical naked,
> dragging themselves through the negro streets at dawn looking for an
>   angry fix . . .

The long, incantatory lines of Ginsberg's "Howl" convey tremendous energy. The syntax—non-standard at times, often startling, but always understandable—forces the mind to move quickly, as if accelerating down a waterslide, the words gathering energy as they go.

3. Rhythmic energy

Life on earth is rhythmic, from the slow rhythm of seasons to the quicker rhythm of the heart. In a good poem, we feel the pulse of the poet's life. No wonder rhythm is a prime source of poetic energy.

Poems in fixed meter come pre-supplied with rhythmic energy. But free verse can convey as much energy, or more. See how, in "They Feed They Lion," Philip Levine generates a rolling, rageful energy that suits its subject perfectly.

> Out of burlap sacks, out of bearing butter,
> Out of black bean and wet slate bread,
> Out of the acids of rage, the candor of tar,
> Out of creosote, gasoline, drive shafts, wooden dollies,
> They lion grow . . .[255]

4. Formal energy

Skillfully used, rhyme and meter bring rhythmic, syntactic, and lexical energy to a poem. The reader's rhythmic expectations, dexterously thwarted or fulfilled, add extra interest to the work. The need to rhyme in meter encourages syntax and word choice touched by the magic of serendipity.

In the sonnet "Twenty Questions," Maura Stanton adds rhythmic energy with her quirky pentameter, and boosts reader interest with unexpected rhymes to go with unexpected questions.

> Who wrote *Heart of Darkness*? And what's the name
> Of Dale Evan's horse? Why did thieves steal
> Charlie Chaplin's corpse? Can you explain

---

255 Philip Levine, "They Feed They Lion," in *Contemporary American Poetry*, 313.

Hieroglyphs in shells? How do you feel?
How many grains of (popcorn, rice, sand) fill
This container? Why did they auction off
Maria Callas's underwear? Would you like a pill? . . .[256]

Cecilia Woloch uses the pantoum's pattern of repetition, along with galloping anapests, to evoke the exuberance of horses and newly sexualized hearts.

One night, bareback and young, we rode through the woods
and the woods were on fire—
two borrowed horses, two local boys
whose waists we clung to, my sister and I

and the woods were on fire—
the pounding of hooves and the smell of smoke and the sharp sweat of boys
whose waists we clung to, my sister and I
as we rode toward flame with the sky in our mouths—. . .[257]

5. Opening energy

In popular fiction, readers drop directly into dramatic situations: A reporter starts to interview a vampire; a city is covered by an impenetrable, transparent dome. In poems, an intriguing title and/or first sentence works in the same way, conveying energy from poet to reader by stoking the reader's curiosity. Steve Kowit's "Hell" begins, "I died and went to hell, and it was nothing like LA."[258] Stephen Dobyns's "The Pony Express" begins, "Some would have you think the Pony Express / is dead. Don't believe it. They're only waiting."[259]

Most readers, I suspect, will want to know what happens next.

6. Conceptual energy

A fresh and original concept or premise can pump a lot of energy into a poem. Warned not to leave matches out ". . . because the mice / might get

256 Maura Stanton, "Twenty Questions," in *Special Orders* (Chicago: University of Illinois Press, 2008): 39.
257 Cecilia Woloch, "Bareback Pantoum," in *The Best American Poetry 2005*, ed. Paul Muldoon and David Lehman (New York: Scribner Poetry, 2005): 146–147.
258 Steve Kowit, "Hell," in *Stand Up Poetry: An Expanded Anthology*, 194.
259 Stephen Dobyns, "The Pony Express," in *Stand Up Poetry: An Expanded Anthology*, 72–73.

into them and start a fire,"[260] the speaker in Billy Collins's "The Country"
portrays the mouse as a rodent Prometheus.

In the bitterly ironic "Letter to my Assailant," Suzanne Lummis depicts an attempted rape as just another failed relationship.

> We leapt from each other
> like two hares released from a trap. Oh, oh,
> something's not right between men and women.
> Perhaps we talked too much,
> or did we leave too much unsaid? . . .
>
> I never intended
> all this to become blurred in my memory,
> to confuse you with other men.[261]

7. Narrative energy

In fiction or poetry, the energy of a good story—engaging plot, setting,
characters—creates a strong urge to read more. The energy of conflict—
someone wants something, but is blocked from getting it—is evident in
these famous lines:

> And indeed there will be time
> To wonder, "Do I dare?" and, "Do I dare?"
> Time to turn back and descend the stair
> With a bald spot in the middle of my hair—
> . . .
> Do I dare
> Disturb the universe?
> In a minute there is time
> For decisions and revisions which a minute will reverse. . . .[262]

---

260 Billy Collins, "The Country," in *Poets of the New Century*, 28–29.

261 Suzanne Lummis, "Letter To My Assailant," in *Stand Up Poetry: An Expanded Anthology*, 210–11.

262 T. S. Eliot, "The Love Song of J. Alfred Prufrock," in *The Norton Anthology of Modern Poetry*, 2nd Edition, ed. Richard Ellmann and Robert O'Clair (New York: W.W. Norton & Company, 1973): 482–85.

8. Lyric energy

Like a constant fortissimo, uninterrupted lyricism can pall. Even "Fern Hill" bolsters its lyric energy with narrative. Still, Thomas's lines show that, properly supported, lyricism remains the tenor in poetry's opera: superstar of the poetic show.

> Now as I was young and easy under the apple boughs
> About the lilting house and happy as the grass was green
>   The night above the dingle starry,
>   Time let me hail and climb
>   Golden in the heydays of his eyes. . . .[263]

9. Erotic energy

Just as in non-literary life, the erotic brings a powerful charge to poetry. "Give me the lover who yanks open the door / of his house and presses me to the wall / in the dim hallway, and keeps me there until I'm drenched / and shaking . . ." says a breathless Kim Addonizio in "For Desire."[264]

"They don't want to stop. They can't stop. / They've been going at it for days now, / for hours, for months, for years. He's on top / of her. She's on top of him. He's licking / her between the legs . . ."[265] writes Catherine Bowman in "Demographics."

The energy of desire is transformed into the energy of words.

10. Emotional energy

Strong emotion (coupled, of course, with good technique) guarantees a gusher of poetic energy. If Ezra Pound is right that "Only emotion endures," Yusef Komunyakaa's "Facing It," which contains one of the most moving yet understated endings in contemporary poetry, is going to last for a long time.

> . . . A white vet's image floats
> closer to me, then his pale eyes
> look through mine. I'm a window.
> He's lost his right arm
> inside the stone. In the black mirror

---

263 Dylan Thomas, "Fern Hill," in *The Norton Anthology of Modern Poetry*, 925–26.
264 Addonizio, "For Desire," in *Stand Up Poetry: An Expanded Anthology*, 1.
265 Catherine Bowman, "Demographics," in *Stand Up Poetry: An Expanded Anthology*, 25–26.

a woman's trying to erase names:
No, she's brushing a boy's hair."[266]

11. Intellectual energy

By "intellectual," I mean more than just "learning"; I mean raw brain-power—the sense, imparted to the reader, that the writer is able to think as well as feel.

John Donne's "A Valediction: Forbidding Mourning," with its famous image of the compass, is a classic display of intellectual energy. Lynn Emanuel's book *Then, Suddenly*[267] has been justly praised for intellectual punch. Matthea Harvey shows intellectual energy in her deft leaps from association to association. And Robert Pinsky's "Samurai Song" displays mathematical precision as well as wit and inventiveness in the Samurai's carefully chosen antidotes to what he lacks.

> When I had no roof I made
> Audacity my roof. When I had
> No supper my eyes dined.
>
> When I had no eyes I listened.
> When I had no ears I thought.
> When I had no thought I waited. . . .[268]

12. Scholarly energy

Interesting facts, artfully introduced, enhance poetic energy. Peter Johnson mixes his own lively associations with historical facts from the lives of Socrates, Nero, Freud, Hemingway, Malcolm X, and others to create imaginative and evocative prose poetry, as in this excerpt from "Samuel Johnson."

> The 18th century, thank God there's still a God—Order, Design, Right Reason not yet gone left. . . . Later, I tell Johnson I'm homesick, but he offers this explanation: "Long intervals of pleasure dissipate attention and weaken constancy." And how right he is! . . . I look to Johnson for solace, but he laughs, pinching wheat-

---

266 Yusef Konunyakaa, "Facing It," in *The Oxford Book of American Poetry*, ed. David Lehman (Oxford: Oxford University Press, 2006): 1035.
267 Lynn Emanuel, *Then, Suddenly* (Pittsburgh: University of Pittsburgh Press, 1999).
268 Robert Pinsky, "Samurai Song," in *Poets of the New Century*, 268–69.

stained vermin from under my wig, soberly addressing one at close range. "And
thee," he says, "I shall name Boswell."[269]

13. Imagistic energy

Studies of the brain show that imagery triggers responses much like what
happens in the presence of the imaged thing (hence the Writer's Workshop
Commandments "Show, don't tell"; "Appeal to the senses"; "Use concrete
imagery"). Advertisers use imagery to make us hungry. Pornographers use
it to make us horny. Poets use it to energize their poetry.

> I don't know what the horned lizard has to live for,
> Skittering over the sun-irritated sand, scraping
> The hot dusty brambles. It never sees anything but gravel
> And grit, thorns and stickery insects, the towering
> Creosote bush, the ocotillo and its whiplike
> Branches, the severe edges of the Spanish dagger....[270]

14. Imaginative energy

Like the flesh, the imagination loves stimulation. The creation of unex-
plored imaginative worlds is a great antidote to boredom, letting us live
with new bodies, and see with new eyes.

In "Adam and Eve's Dog,"[271] Richard Garcia introduces a new and
winning character to the Garden of Eden. Dean Young, by juxtaposing
one surprising statement with another in the excerpt below, gives readers
a new take on our "normal" world.

> ... One reason to have sex is to help a stranger
> get in touch with his or her animal being
> even if it's a crayfish.
> In the kitchen the rotisserie was laboring,
> either the chicken was too fat
> or it was tuckering out. Oddly,
> I didn't feel bad for Franklin Delano

269 Peter Johnson, "Samuel Johnson," in *Rants and Raves* (Buffalo: White Pine Press, 2010): 40.
270 Pattiann Rogers, "Justification of the Horned Lizard," in *Stand Up Poetry: An Expanded
Anthology*, 244–45.
271 Richard Garcia, "Adam and Eve's Dog," in *The Persistence of Objects* (Rochester: BOA
Editions, 2006): 69–70.

even though he looked jaunty and vulnerable
in his wheelchair in the margin of the dictionary. . . .[272]

15. Metaphoric energy

Aristotle claimed that metaphor is "the one thing that cannot be learned from others. It is also a mark of genius." Robert Frost said, "Metaphor is the whole of poetry." Metaphor may well exemplify an early, pre-verbal mode of thought. In any case, strong metaphors clarify the primal link between all things. In their light, the world seems rediscovered, renewed, re-energized, as in this excerpt from Lucia Perillo's "The Crows Start Demanding Royalties."

> . . . witness how, when they walk, their heads jerk
> back and forth like rifle bolts.
> How they heave their shoulders into each stride
> as if they hoped that by some chance
> new bones there would come popping out
> with a boxing glove on the end of each.
>
> Little Elvises, the hairdo slicked
> with too much grease . . .[273]

16. Energy of surprise

People read to be surprised. Every good poem is full of unexpected words, images, metaphors, and occurrences that give the brain a jolt, experienced as interest/energy.

Thomas Lux, in his poem "Plague Victims Catapulted Over Walls Into Besieged City," surprises with a macabre fact of medieval warfare, surprises again by humanizing the corpse-bombs with names and occupations, then arrives at this poignant and startling conclusion:

> . . . the Hatter Twins, both at once, soar
> over the parapet, little Tommy's elbow bent
> as in a salute,
> and his sister, Mathilde, she follows him,

---

272 Dean Young, "Sex With Strangers," in *Primitive Mentor* (Pittsburgh: University of Pittsburgh Press, 2008): 35–36.
273 Perillo, "The Crows Start Demanding Royalties," in *Luck Is Luck*, 10.

> arms outstretched, through the air,
> just as she did on earth.[274]

In the tender image of a little girl trying to embrace a reluctant brother, we recover the humanity of these early germ-warfare "bombs," and gain an unexpected sense of the preciousness of our own lives.

17. Humorous energy

Well-known as a marker of intelligence, humor draws on many other energies: surprise, imagination, metaphor, etc. People enjoy humor even—or especially—in the midst of tragedies. Intensely subversive, humor is an effective way to deal with postmodern concerns—slipperiness of language and identity, tendency of statements to deconstruct themselves, etc.—while keeping the reader entertained. It's a great force of redemption in human life, lifting our spirits even as it brings us the bad news.

Russell Edson's "The Automobile" lets us laugh at what otherwise might make us cry.

> . . . The son shows father an ignition key. See, here is a special penis which does with the automobile as the man with the woman; and the automobile gives birth to a place far from this place, dropping its puppy miles as it goes.

> Does that make me a grandfather? said father.

> That makes you where you are when I am far away, said the son. . . .[275]

17A. Satiric energy. By spotlighting human foibles and follies, satire helps us gain, at least briefly, the upper hand. In "I'm Dealing with My Pain," Denise Duhamel satirizes psychobabble, while speaking of serious psychological pain.

> He's about 300 pounds and knows martial arts, boxing, and wrestling—both the real and the fake kind. So I never know when I'm thrown to the ground or hurled against the ropes of a boxing ring fence (who can guess when he'll

274 Thomas Lux, "Plague Victims Catapulted Over Walls Into Besieged City," in *The Street of Clocks* (Boston: Houghton Mifflin Company, 2001): 3.
275 Russell Edson, "The Automobile," in *Stand Up Poetry: An Expanded Anthology*, 86.

surprise me with a punch next?) if the ache in my back is real or cartoon, if my bruises will stay or wash off like kiddie tattoos.[276]

18. Allusive energy

Literary allusion taps the energy of previous art, either by referring to or recapitulating it, as in Edward Field's "The Bride of Frankenstein."[277] For energy to flow optimally from poet to reader, though, the allusion must be recognized. This can be a problem, now that readers don't share a common knowledge-base. Still, Ron Koertge can use his reader's knowledge of The Man of Steel to energize an epistolary poem from Lois Lane:

> Dear Superman
>
> I know you think that things
> will always be the same: I'll rinse
> out your tights, kiss you good-bye
> at the window, and every few weeks
> get kidnapped by some stellar goons. . . .[278]

19. Energy of accretion

A big part of the art of poetry is providing just enough information, and no more. Many weak poems are overlong. But sometimes more is more. Sometimes, as in Whitman's "Song of Myself," poems accumulate energy as they go.

David Kirby dazzles with his ability to juggle many balls at the same time. In poems such as "The Search for Baby Combover," "I Think Stan Done It," and "Meetings with Remarkable Men,"[279] he layers story on story, each adding to the energy of previous ones, even as it contributes its own.

20. Antisocial energy

People are fascinated by the transgressive, the criminal, the *bad*. Just as Satan powers *Paradise Lost*, and Dracula's heirs continue to inspire books and films, so the pugnacious speaker in Philip Levine's "The Fox"[280] is

---

276 Denise Duhamel, "I'm Dealing With My Pain," in *Stand Up Poetry: An Expanded Anthology*, 77.

277 Edward Field, "The Bride of Frankenstein," in *Stand Up Poetry: An Expanded Anthology*, 99–100.

278 Ron Koertge, "Dear Superman," in *Stand Up Poetry: An Expanded Anthology*, 191.

279 Kirby, *The House on Boulevard St.*

280 Philip Levine, "The Fox," in *One for the Rose* (New York: Atheneum, 1982).

more interesting than a polite, accommodating man would be. Jeffrey Harrison's transgression in "Fork" is not on the scale of Satan's, but it satisfies the human urge for revenge.

> I stole a fork, slipping it into the pocket of my jeans,
> then hummed with inward glee the rest of the evening
> to feel its sharp tines pressing against my thigh
> as we sat around you in your dark paneled study
> listening to you blather on about your latest prize....[281]

20A. Violent energy. *Homo sapiens* is an aggressive animal, fascinated by violence, both physical and verbal. Just as children flock to a fight at school, readers are drawn to work that addresses our violent side—releasing, in the act, a rush of primal energy.

Tony Hoagland's "Lawrence" is energized by the power of invective and imagined mayhem.

> I resolve, if the occasion should recur,
> to uncheck my tongue and say, "I love the spectacle
> of maggots condescending to a corpse,"
>
> ...
>
> Or maybe I'll just take the shortcut
> between the spirit and the flesh
> and punch someone in the face ...[282]

21. Anxious energy

It's not surprising, in our Age of Anxiety, that anxiety powers many poems. The modern world spawns endless insecurities, and gives us leisure to indulge in and embellish them. In "Wrong Poem," Mark Halliday satirizes and dramatizes anxious self absorption in the world of poetry, and the world at large.

> Not *this* poem, *your* poem, your poem is the one,
> not this poem, this is not what you want,

---

281 Jeffrey Harrison, "Fork," in *Incomplete Knowledge* (New York: Four Way Books, 2006): 9–11.
282 Tony Hoagland, "Lawrence," in *Stand Up Poetry: An Expanded Anthology*, 157–58.

though it seemed refreshing for a second
this poem will not feed you but only
increase your hunger. Already you don't quite like it
and this trend will only intensify.
Is intensify the right verb?
Is hunger the right metaphor?
Neither feels quite right to you, of course not, because
the poem you need is yours. . . .[283]

22. Tender energy

Energy doesn't have to be loud or aggressive. The poems of Edward Hirsch are frequently suffused with the energy of compassion and tenderness. His poem "Special Orders" is a poignant portrait of a man willing to humble himself for the sake of his family, but also simply to do a good job—"my father, who wanted your business / would squat down at your side / and sketch you a container for it."[284]

In "A Partial History of My Stupidity," Hirsch expresses compassion, regret, and apology toward all those who suffer, and even toward the God he is unable to accept.

> So I walked on—distracted, lost in thought—
> and forgot to attend to those who suffered
> far away, nearby.
>
> Forgive me, faith, for never having any.
>
> I did not believe in God,
> who eluded me.[285]

23. Playful energy

High spirits are treated with condescension in some literary circles, as if feeling good were a sign of shallowness.[286] Yet what would Frank O'Hara's poems be without their exuberant play? How, if he hadn't given high spir-

---

283 Mark Halliday, "Wrong Poem," in *Poets of the New Century*, 127–28.
284 Edward Hirsch, "Special Orders," in *Special Orders* (New York: Alfred A. Knopf, 2008): 3.
285 Ibid., 33.
286 Depressive energy is an oxymoron. For the soul to be roused to poetry, depression must, at least briefly, lift.

its free rein, would James Tate have come up with poems like "Teaching the Ape to Write Poems," or "Goodtime Jesus"?

> . . . It was a beautiful day. How 'bout some coffee? Don't mind if I do. Take a little ride on my donkey, I love that donkey. Hell, I love everybody.[287]

24. Energy of personality

Some people seem to have an extra-hot furnace burning inside. Their feelings are strong, their experiences vivid. These people can be extroverted or introverted, quiet and polite, or loud and obstreperous; they may be leaders or loners. But if such people can express their inner power in words, those words will carry a strong charge of energy, made stronger still if the personality is unusual or unique.

Such powerful personalities will almost certainly evoke a strong reader response.[288] I vividly remember borrowing Sharon Olds's *Satan Says* from a friend in the early 1980s. "I've never seen anything like this," I thought and, exhilarated, read the book straight through.

25. Finishing energy

Like a boxer with a killer instinct, some poets knock the reader out with a last line that could not have been predicted, but seems inevitable, once it arrives.

I've already praised the endings of Komunyakaa's "Facing It," and Lux's "Plague Victims Catapulted Over Walls Into Besieged City." Mark Strand's well-known "Keeping Things Whole" wraps up a series of stark statements of alienation with a last sentence that confirms the speaker's aloneness, but turns his own failure-to-belong into something positive for the rest of the world: "I move to keep things whole."[289]

26. Aha! energy

This is what poets are ultimately after: the sudden spark that illuminates the poem, and life itself. Though it often comes—*if* it comes—near the end of a poem, it can arrive at any time. Closely related to metaphor, aha! energy explodes with the discovery—surprising to the poet as to the reader—"This is the poem's truth! This is what it's all about!"

---

287 Tate, "Goodtime Jesus," in *Selected Poems*, 177.

288 Sometimes the response will not be positive.

289 Mark Strand, "Keeping Things Whole," in *Contemporary American Poetry*, 529.

William Trowbridge's "Coach Said" seems to be a high school coach's rant to his team about the imagined perils of drinking water during practice. As such, the poem is realistic, idiomatically precise, convincingly laughable. Then, in the last four lines, the aha! arrives.

> Don't expect to be some Romeo stud, who thinks
> his little cheerleader won't spit on him when he's down.
> I could tell you some things, but just remember this:
> It ain't gonna be like last year. No goddamn water.[290]

In these lines—especially "It ain't gonna be like last year"—we understand that the coach is talking about himself: his failures and disappointments, the year-after-year repetition of which he thinks he can stop, for himself and the boys, if he instills enough fear and discipline. As what was funny becomes poignant, even tragic, for all concerned, the poem's energy level—already more than sufficient—shoots higher still.

With so many ways to impart energy, we might assume that most poems would be packed with it. Yet some poets, for theoretical and/or emotional reasons, eschew the usual sources. In theory, avant-garde qualities such as impermeability, indeterminacy, opacity, attention-scattering, fragmentation, and discontinuity impart their own energy and even ecstasy (*jouissance*); in practice, they often block energy from making the writer-to-reader leap.

There are also many ways to quash poetic energy unintentionally.

1. Craft/editing issues
Poor word choice, over- and under-writing, dead wood, cliché, lack of concrete imagery, inept figurative language, problems with structure—all such writing workshop issues can keep energy from reaching the reader, and vitiate what does squeak through.

2. Lack of clarity
The way a dust cloud blocks light, lack of clarity blocks the transfer of verbal energy.

---

290 William Trowbridge, "Coach Said," in *Ship of Fool* (Pasadena: Red Hen Press, 2011): 50.

3. Obviousness

If what the poet says is commonplace, or if the reader sees where the poem will end before it arrives, there will be little of the energy-release that makes reading enjoyable. No matter how much energy the poet pumps in, it leaks out instantly.

4. Poor pacing

Good fishermen know that if they let their line go slack, their fish will likely get away. When a poem's lines go slack, energy escapes; the reader gets away. Good writing keeps readers curious, feeding them information exactly when they need it—not after; not before.

4A. Stasis. Some poems start out energetically, then stall. Individual lines may be good, but there is no sense of building, no heightened tension, no dramatic development. The poem continues in a monotone, leaking more energy the longer it goes on.

5. Puffery

The true subject of some poems is the essential wonderfulness—moral, intellectual, political, temperamental—of the poet. This may energize the poet, but kills the poem.

5A. Pedantry. Poets who flaunt learning the way rappers flaunt rap sheets and gold chains, clutter their poems and sap their energy.

6. Distancing

Poets may affect an "objective" stance meant to mute or obliterate the poet's personality. Human thought, though, is always subjective. Attempts to remove personality from a poem remove life-energy, and kill the poem.

7. Willed energy

Some poems are acts of will, forced out by the writer's wish to produce, but not energized by artistic discovery. A willed poem is like a Diet Coke: the brain may think that it's drinking "the real thing," but receives no usable energy.

8. Low or no stakes

Increasing numbers of poets write from a stance of hip, knowing, world-weariness, producing work so ironized, elliptical, devoid of honest human engagement as to be—even when witty and/or inventive—meaningless. Such poems may mimic the movements of imagination; but with little or no recognizable link to the poet's or the reader's inner life, they have no viable source of energy.

9. Low energy in, low energy out

Just as some people are vibrant and strong, some seem weak, indistinct, tentative, wan.[291] Poems arising from such personalities are unlikely to have much energy. This problem, I suspect, causes most of the other ones.

On the other hand, poets who *have* energy may believe that to express it is unseemly, unsophisticated, immature, as well as, in some cases, too personally revealing. Unconsciously or not, such poets fear their own energy, and banish it from their poems. The result may be a display of inauthentic force, or a prim, pale poetry that shows the poet as morally, emotionally, and intellectually unimpeachable, but leaves the poem de-energized—moribund, if not dead.

Energy is, of course, in the mind of the reader. What seems high-energy to one may seem disagreeable frenzy to another; what strikes Reader A as low-energy may be enough to exhilarate Reader B. Some people like Mantovani; some like Motorhead.

In any case, if poets care about their audience, they need to write poems that *live.* Even the most avid American readers generally read no poetry. That's doubly sad, since exciting poems are being written every day. Dead poems have not driven out living ones, as per Gresham's Law; but living poems may be buried under piles of corpses. If—to use a less gruesome metaphor—would-be poetry readers must search for needles in haystacks, and aren't even sure that those needles exist, most will give up.

I don't expect poetry to be as popular as *Judge Judy* or Monday Night Football; but it could be more popular than it is. Poetry has much to offer the twenty-first century reader. It can tell a story with precision and speed, explore and dramatize psychological states, map the path of awareness, and follow imagination as it leaps, squirms, and flashes through the mind. It can provide moments of clarity akin to $E=mc^2$, and help us to remember them. It can guide us through waking dreams, and dazzle us with metaphor, which renews and revitalizes the world. It can convey the pleasures of voice—including humor and wit—which are akin to

---

291 These may be signs of depression, the defining characteristic of which is debilitating loss of energy.

the pleasures of good conversation. It can help us get more out of life, in the same way that understanding the subtleties of baseball increases enjoyment of the game. It can provide assurance that others have thought and felt as we do. It can rekindle in us the power and joy of naming—the sense of exaltation that makes a two-year-old point at her feet, yell "Shoe," and dance with delight. It can revel with us in the physical sound of words, the delight of onomatopoeia, the sensual feel of *abomination* and *contextual* on the tongue. It can commemorate and concretize experiences that would otherwise be lost, while enhancing empathy, the source of all morality.

To do these things, though, requires a lot of energy. If "general" readers are ever to come back to poetry—to choose a book of poems, let's say, for reading at the beach or on a bus—more poets must access more energy, and get it into poems that will transfer it, unimpeded, to readers' brains and hearts. From there, anything is possible.

The Limits of Indeterminacy:
A Defense of Less Difficult Poetry

You ain't so smart. I been believing in nothing ever since I was born.
—Flannery O'Connor, "Good Country People"

For decades now, American poetry has been under the influence of literary theories arising from, and contributing to, the collapse of fundamental Western "truths." Revolving around concepts of uncertainty and indeterminacy, and borrowing intellectual heft from Science—Heisenberg's Uncertainty Principle; Einstein's Relativity—these essentially nihilistic ideas include the following:

1. There is no God, so there are no absolute standards of good and bad, right and wrong, beautiful and ugly, worthy and unworthy—no standards but those that self-interested humans invent, and impose upon others. Man was not made in God's image, and *human nature* does not exist. The mind is essentially a Blank Slate.

2. Logic and causality are constructs imposed on experience. Any coherent story is an ex post facto organization of chaos. Instead of moving by logical progression, life is a series of non sequiturs governed by Chance. Straightforward narrative[292]—from a single point of view, or even several—distorts reality (if such a thing exists), and is exclusionary and potentially oppressive.

3. Language creates the world as humans know it, and perhaps as it "is." "Reality" is what Language allows us to know.

4. Yet Language is inadequate to map the world, and accurately convey what it finds. Words (signifiers) are slippery, bound loosely, if at all, to what they describe (the signified). A man may say, "Please

---

292 Tony Hoagland has written, with his usual insight and good sense, about the avant-garde's distrust of narrative in "Fear of Narrative and the Skittery Poem of Our Moment," in *Real Sofistikashun*, 173–87.

pass the salt," confident that he will receive what he requests; but to a sophisticated thinker, this is the bliss of ignorance.

Furthermore, when corrupted—as it has been—by exploitive political systems, Language forfeits what slight ability to communicate it might have had.

5. The concept of "I" is far less stable than the rock of Gibraltar, which is far less stable than it might be. "I" is a fiction, made up of many simultaneously operating, constantly changing partial- and pseudo-"I"s. The "self" is at least as slippery as any other noun. The unified self is a myth.

6. Since any statement can be shown to imply its opposite, *meaning* is meaningless.

7. Since all literary standards are arbitrary and biased, it is unjustifiable to "privilege" one text over another. *Hamlet* is no "better" than *Shack Tramp* or a Huggies ad.

8. Given that everything that can be said is already contained in Language ("always already written," as Barthes says), the author has little to do with the creation of texts, and may even be said to be "dead."

9. Any attempt by an author to impose a particular point of view, narrative structure, or emotional response upon the reader not only falsifies human experience, but constitutes intellectual fascism. Authors, to the extent that they exist, have no special authority. Their sole function is to pull from the ether "already written" texts to be interpreted as readers see fit.

Poems influenced by these ideas have been labeled "difficult," "experimental," "avant-garde," "L=A=N=G=U=A=G=E," "postmodern," "post-postmodern," "challenging," "dissociative," "elusive," "elliptical," as well as less flattering names. Attempting to embody these ideas—and not to embody "under-theorized," "unproblematized" ones—poets have replaced traditional development-of-subjects with non sequiturs, and orchestration-of-effects with randomness. They have embraced textual self-consciousness, exposing their technique. They have rejected "sincerity" as unsophisticated and false. They have fostered emotional distance and disengagement. They have embraced psychological dislocation, trying to disguise or remove personality from their work. They have intentionally bored the reader, hoping to jolt him/her into a new understanding and consciousness. They have piled irony on irony, and stopped even trying to reach the elusive and vanishing "general reader." They have thwarted such readers' desire to lose themselves in what John Gardner called reading's "waking dream," offering texts so indeterminate that readers must abandon all expectations for meaning and sense, in hopes of experiencing an orgasmic *jouissance.* They have rejected mimesis and theme, while elevating invention and surprise.[293]

Yet, many of the scientific/philosophical ideas that set the Difficult ball rolling are partly or wholly untrue. Even when they *are* true, the consequences for poetry are much less extreme than has been supposed. The sky, as it turns out, is not falling; it has just tilted a bit.

Literary theories are very different from scientific ones. A scientific theory must be testable. To be accepted as true, that truth must be shown objectively, and replicably, in the physical world. Psychoanalytic theory, for instance, succeeds as science only to the extent that it accurately and verifiably explains the working of the mind.

Literary theories are not testable. (If they are, they become scientific theories.) To gain academic acceptance, a literary theory need only appeal to other literary theorists. In the world of literary studies, psychoanalytic theory succeeds if it helps scholars to say fresh things about texts. Whether it, and conclusions reached through it, are "true" is beside the point—especially if objective truth is unattainable, and likely a myth.

Still, if the theories underpinning works of art misrepresent how human brains process that art, those brains may well reject the art. If the worldview underlying a work of art proves to be false, that art may become as irrelevant as phlogiston.

With that in mind, let's look more closely at the principles listed above.

Uncertainty/Indeterminacy. Heisenberg's Uncertainty Principle states that we cannot know both the momentum and position of a quantum particle at the same time. This principle operates at full strength only in the ultra-tiny world of quantum mechanics; yet it has been taken to mean that humans can't know much of anything.

Yes, there is uncertainty in the human-scale world. There is no denying the strong influence of Chance. Yet, from the fact that we will die, to the strong likelihood that our house will be, tonight, where we left it this

---

293 More recently, in pursuit of what Stephen Burt has labeled "The New Thing" *Boston Review* (May/June 2009), some have abandoned invention and high energy in favor of a stripped-down, hermetic, near-anorexic concreteness based on W. C. Williams's "No ideas but in things."

morning, our world is not so unpredictable. Even when we can't know absolutely, we can often know to a high degree of certainty.

Relativity. Einstein's Theories of Relativity state that, since an absolute space-time coordinate system does not exist, there can be no absolute position in space and time—i.e., position is relative. Furthermore, relative to an observer moving near the speed of light, both time and space are altered. Einstein's theories do not mean that everything is relative, and nothing is certain. In Einstein's universe, the speed of light is *absolutely* certain.

No God. The God proposition is unprovable either way. Yet, even though not absolute or supernaturally decreed, ethical and aesthetic standards exist. Proof continues to accumulate that basic moral and aesthetic principles are products of evolution. Babies seem to come pre-equipped with a sense of justice[294] and beauty, among other things. Though "human nature" is plastic within limits, it too exists. Every culture creates laws and customs to enforce its beliefs. The fact that these beliefs aren't universal and unassailable does not make them less relevant to human lives or art.

No logic or causality. Logic is fallible, as logic itself can prove. But the most fallible logic is the formal kind. What Freud called the *Unconscious* uses a logic that incorporates more (and more complex) information, and processes it more quickly than the formal kind. Some people call this *intuition*.

The human brain evolved logic to help it survive in the world.[295] From our perspective, events move from beginning to end, via cause and effect. Our brains process information that way. The fact that the quantum world is ruled by probability does not mean that our lives, as we experience them, are too. Chance may disrupt our best-laid plans. Still, in our macro-world, causes and effects are real. If you doubt this, stomp your bare foot on an upturned tack.

Language creates the world. I remember my undergraduate excitement on encountering Whorf's notion that the language we speak dictates how we see the world, and maybe even what exists. The idea that Eskimos see many types of snow, while we see just a few, has instant appeal. For those of us who love and specialize in language, it's especially pleasing to think the world exists because of what we're expert in.

---

294 Old Testament-style: eye for an eye.

295 Even extremely Difficult poets defend their practices in logical essays, as if their theories apply only when making art.

That doesn't make it true. Neuroscientist V. S. Ramachandran tells of an Amazonian tribe with no word but "many" for numbers greater than three. Yet tests showed that members of the lexically challenged tribe dealt with large numbers as well as members of tribes who did have words for larger numbers.[296]

Animals' brains serve them well without language. If our earliest hominid ancestors had needed language, we wouldn't be here today. Evidence supports the existence of a world independent of language or observation—a "reality" (from our perspective) that operates according to knowable Laws. This is the world that Language describes, and in which it is a valuable survival tool.

Failure of language. Though Language has been credited with creating the world, some thinkers lament its inadequacy to describe that world. But the problem has been overstated—mightily! Just because there are many words for what we call *watermelon* does not mean that language has a problem. Nor does the fact that watermelons vary in color, shape, and taste render the word meaningless. If I say *watermelon*, each English speaker who hears will call up a slightly different mental image; but all who know the word will know what I mean. Similarly, if I say, "Look behind you," or "I left five hundred dollars for you under that rock," any competent English speaker will know what to do. Words may squirm, but we can easily hold on.

The poet's job has always been to make words express more than seems possible. Imagery helps. Metaphor helps. "Music" helps. Describing what "words can't describe" is what good poets do!

As for the corruption of Language by "the system"—rather than throw up their hands, or tear sense and syntax limb-from-limb, the best writers prove the problems surmountable in plain English. (Or Mandarin. Or Swahili.) If poets aren't able to out-express politicians and ad-men, they should choose another line of work.

Unstable "I." It's true that normal people change personae according to their audience. It's also true that people who lack self-knowledge often surprise themselves. But psychological research has shown that personal-

---

296 New Age guru Leonard Orr, who popularized the therapeutic technique known as Rebirthing, has called death "a self-fulfilling prophecy." If we had no word for death, I've heard him state, we would not think of it, and it wouldn't exist. At 75, Orr is still alive and kicking. We'll have to wait and see.

ity is remarkably stable after about age six.[297] Philosophers' romance with the "unstable self" arises, I suspect, from a tendency to romanticize psychopathology, and from fear of biological determinism.

Existentialists contend that we choose, instant to instant, who we are. *I'm a drug addict. Now I choose not to be. Uh-oh, I just did drugs, so I'm an addict again. Now, I choose not to do drugs anymore, so I'm not an addict.* Etc. It's an appealing notion, but ignores biology, the imperatives of which create a genuine *I*, and can make a mere verbal decision as futile as rowing into a hurricane.

Poets can, of course, write from different perspectives within a poem. They can try to write from no personality at all. But rather than reach a deeper understanding of the shaky ontological nature of the self and/ or the world, most readers will likely reject the speaker of such poems as fraudulent, and not worth listening to.

"Meaning" as meaningless. Because our lives lack cosmic Meaning does not mean they lack meaning *to us.* Ask the parents of a longed-for baby if the new life lacks meaning.

Thank Deconstruction for the notion that we can't say "what we mean" without also saying (and meaning) its opposite—a notion that has metastasized into the belief that no one can have anything meaningful to say, and couldn't say it if he/she had. Deconstruction, while clever, is essentially playful sophistry: a verbal game that reveals more about the ingenuity of the deconstructionist and the limits of lock-step logic than about our friend "reality." If I tell a disruptive student, "Please be quiet," I'm not simultaneously asking him to continue speaking, as he will learn if he tests me.

As intellectual play, and a way to expose contradictions—some genuine, some not—Deconstruction can be fun. But quirks in language and lock-step logic—Zeno's paradoxes are early examples—do not reveal a true breakdown of meaning.

All texts are created equal. I could offer arguments such as "quality of mind" and "clarity of vision," trying to disprove this statement. But preferring Keats to a Huggies ad is, finally, a matter of taste; and as another text tells us, there's no arguing that. Still, writers are free to choose their own standards, and to write as if those standards arrived from On High.

---

297 On a trip to my childhood home, I found a stash of my grade school papers, and was amazed to find that, in the seventh grade, I already sounded just like me.

Author as corpse. People who envy authors may delight in reports of their demise. But, in the words of one author, pseudonymed Twain, this demise has been "greatly exaggerated."

Because the number of sayable things isn't infinite, it does not follow that everything that can be said is "always already written." From a human's finite perspective, a very, very large number of possible utterances is as good as infinite. Given that even to repeat the same word is not to say the same thing every time, it's clear that every possible meaning could not have been expressed, much less written, even on a blackboard as large as the universe. Barthes's phrase exemplifies his playfulness with texts. But even if everything were "always already written," no brain could hold it all; so authors can still create, for themselves and their audience, something that wasn't there before.

Author as Hitler. In the post-Holocaust world, few words carry the opprobrium of *fascist.* Yet not all strong leaders are bad. If I'm lost in a jungle, and find someone—even an autocrat—who knows the way out, I'm not oppressed if I choose to follow her or him. By putting myself into an author's hands, I don't accept psychic slavery; I agree to follow, temporarily and for my own pleasure, another consciousness.

A Defense of Less Difficult Poetry

Right or wrong, the theories discussed above have sparked excellent poems. I hope it's clear, though, that Difficult poems are not the inevitable outcome of "advances" in our theoretical understanding of the world. To write Difficult is not a philosophical necessity, but an aesthetic choice.

As Tony Hoagland points out, there are:

> ... two well-known descriptions of what a poem is, and does, one by Wordsworth, one by Stevens:
>
> TYPE A: Poetry is the spontaneous overflow of powerful feelings; it takes its origin from emotion recollected in tranquility.
>
> TYPE B: The poem must resist the intelligence / Almost successfully.[298]

---

298 Tony Hoagland, "Recognition, Vertigo, and Passionate Worldliness," *Poetry Magazine* (September 2010).

Type B poems are, by definition, Difficult. Type A poems may not be easy, but they are less Difficult. Not surprisingly, these types of poems attract different types of readers.[299]

Type A readers—once the norm—"want to experience a kind of clarification; to feel and see deeply into the world that they inhabit."[300] They want poetry "that characterizes and clarifies human nature,"[301] and helps them to live. Though they may know literary theory inside and out, they don't want to be self-conscious when they read. They love "the movie in the mind," the "waking dream" that they experience when lost in a text. They see reading as a chance to live by proxy, gaining experiences almost as vivid as real life. They want to meet fascinating people, and inhabit fascinating minds. "Do with me what you will," they tell the poet. "Just don't bore me."

Most avid readers start as Type A. Many remain there happily. But others, over time, mutate toward Type B.

Type B readers want poems that "disrupt or rearrange consciousness," creating "a condition of not-entirely understanding."[302] They typically want to be self-conscious when they read. They mistrust the waking dream, the movie-in-the-mind, and may scorn such pleasures as naive. Rather than "Take me, I'm yours," their attitude toward the poet is, "I know your tricks. You can't seduce me." Refusing to be passive recipients of any poet's thoughts, they demand to co-create meaning. They're likely to be very aware of literary theory, and to accept its premises. Type B readers want poetry to challenge the limits of their intellect.

For purposes of this discussion, I will call poets who write for Type B readers "Difficult." Since most poetry strikes most contemporary readers as at least somewhat difficult, I will call poets who write for Type A readers, "Less Difficult."[303]

Like Beauty, Difficulty is in the eye of the beholder. "The Love Song of J. Alfred Prufrock" seemed Difficult when it appeared. Now, to anyone familiar with contemporary poetry, it's not difficult at all.

---

299 Of course, there is much overlap.

300 Hoagland, "Recognition, Vertigo, and Passionate Worldliness."

301 Ibid.

302 Ibid.

303 Common terms to describe this type of poet include "Accessible," "Reader-friendly," "Hospitable," "Welcoming," and the opposite of Difficult, "Easy." All of these terms have also been used pejoratively.

The Waste Land, for all its familiarity, is still fairly Difficult. Its use of foreign languages and obscure allusions, its changing speakers and lack of transitions make most readers glad for copious footnotes. Yet extended passages of lyric brilliance, and a consistent general tone (gloom and exhaustion, as it happens), mitigate the difficulty.

Ezra Pound's *Cantos* are Difficult for the same reasons as *The Waste Land*, and leavened similarly by lyric brilliance. Pound's allusions and foreign quotations, though, are more obscure than Eliot's. Also, Pound was certifiably insane.

Mention Difficult poetry today, and L=A=N=G=U=A=G=E jumps to mind. The most influential and imitated Difficult poet writing today, though, is probably John Ashbery. His fertility of imagination, as well as his linguistic chops, are formidable. Still, reading his work can be like watching a man write brilliantly on a blackboard with his right hand, while his left, a line or two behind, erases all that's gone before.[304]

A number of poets, termed "Elliptical" by Stephen Burt,[305] write Difficult poems that seem to arise from the mating of L=A=N=G=U=A=G=E poetry with associative riffing like Dean Young's, and wacky wildness like James Tate's.

A pioneer in this style, and one of my favorites, is Mark Levine. His poem "Unemployment (1)" goes like this.

> I had a calling.
> I took the call.
> It was all I could do to follow the voice streaming into me
> Like traffic on the runway where I lay
> Down to gather.
> I had a calling. I heard the geese bleat
> In the firmament as they migrated
> Into the jet's jets.
> And could I have foreseen that falling
> I could have fallen too
> Rather than being sutured to the bottomless
> Freeze-out lake.
> For it is fine to lie within one's borrowed blankets

---

304 I'm not at all sure that he—poetic trickster that he is—would dislike this characterization.
305 Stephen Burt, "The Elliptical Poets," in *Close Calls With Nonsense* (Minneapolis: Graywolf Press, 2009): 345–55.

Looking up at the
Dropped ceiling coming down.
For at the moment I am employed counting the holes
In the sound absorbing tiles
Keeping a running record of the interlocutor's
Chides.
I feel at one with extinction
By my own hand
(Inner hand)
Though once there were many of my kind
Flocking inland, or perhaps
It felt that way.[306]

I enjoy the wordplay in this poem, the vivid imagery, the way one line
of thought branches into another in unpredictable ways. I admire fresh
and evocative phrases such as "the bottomless / Freeze-out lake" and "the
interlocutor's / Chides." I like the ending's strong statement of loss, "once
there were many of my kind / Flocking inland," undercut by, "or perhaps /
It felt that way," acknowledging the subjectivity of human perception. As
to what the poem "means," I doubt that paraphrasable "meaning" is what
Levine is going for. I suspect that the poem "means" itself—no less, no
more. I do know, though, that I could write a longish paper investigating
what it *might* mean.

I admire the work of Susan Wheeler—also labeled "Elliptical"—for its
intelligence, wide-ranging knowledge, and strong self-awareness. Here is
the brief "She's a Pill."

Oh, dangling long sleeves in the Mercurochrome.
Parking her punch on her knees.

I'm not a joiner.

In the night, a visitation, small as a thumb,
enters the sealed house and ascends.

Mother wouldn't have stood for *that* long. Drippy-drooping around

---

306 Mark Levine, "Unemployment (1)," *Poetry Magazine* (July/August 2012).

on heels. Leaving the blue cheese out.[307]

This short poem crackles with interesting words: "Mercurochrome" (dreaded wound-dressing from my childhood); "drippy-drooping" (perfect to describe some people I've known).

"Parking her punch on her knees," seems to imply that someone formidable is sitting with hands in (or close to) her lap. Following that phrase, the differently indented non sequitur "I'm not a joiner" jolts me away from the "she" who is "a pill," into the speaker's consciousness, and one fact (is it a lie?) about herself.

What the "visitation" is, I can't say—though I could speculate at length.

If I had to guess, I'd say this poem is about two sisters, one the speaker, one the pill. I don't have a clear picture of either one; but to provide that is not Wheeler's intent. Instead I get a few fragments of portraiture. If I want more, I must supply it.

My students, when first faced with Difficult poems, often react with outrage. "How can anybody understand this stuff?" they say.

Their outrage increases when I state that Difficult poets write as they do, not because they can't write more clearly, but because *they don't want to.*

Self-described Difficult poet Charles Bernstein asks, "1. Do you find the poem hard to appreciate? 2. Do you find the poem's vocabulary and syntax hard to understand? 3. Are you often struggling with the poem? 4. Does the poem make you feel inadequate or stupid as a reader? 5. Is your imagination being affected by the poem?

"If you answered any of these questions in the affirmative," he says, "you are probably dealing with a difficult poem."[308]

Difficult poetry is, by definition, difficult to read. It doesn't yield to strategies that general readers use. More successful strategies include the following:

Read to enjoy the sound of the language. Savor individual words.

Read for an overall impression. Read several more times for a more definite impression.

---

307 Susan Wheeler, "She's a Pill," in *Meme* (Iowa City: University of Iowa Press, 2012).
308 Charles Bernstein, *Attack of the Difficult Poems* (Chicago: University of Chicago Press, 2011): 3–4.

Give up all expectations, and "have your way with the text," as Barthes might say. Relish your freedom, entering and leaving the text when and where you like; making it mean what you want it to.

In "Close Calls with Nonsense: How to Read and Perhaps Enjoy Very New Poetry,"[309] Stephen Burt offers a list of ways to proceed. These include, "look for a persona and a world, not for an argument or a plot. Enjoy double meanings; don't feel you must choose between them." But Burt's many excellent suggestions require repeated close readings—i.e., *studying* the poem.

To study, though, is not always to enjoy. I like to enjoy the poem first, then study to enjoy it more. Over three hundred years ago, John Dryden complained of poets who give us "a hard nut to break our teeth, without a kernel for our pains." Difficult poetry often requires that we crack the hard nut first, and hope a kernel will be there—that, or insert our own.

Less Difficult poets still abound. But if there is a fight for dominance, the Difficult have grabbed the upper hand. Difficult poets may not be more numerous, but they seem younger than the Less Difficult, their influence growing faster as they flood out of influential graduate schools. They see themselves as more philosophically "with it" than the Less Difficult— more adventurous and hip, their work flashing with panache. Adorned with literary theory, they radiate the glamour of intellectual rebels: stylish, cool, in tune with the latest trends. Many Difficult poets profess boredom with, not to say contempt for, Less Difficult work: too obvious, too easy, too predictable.

I've written mildly Elliptical poems, and can testify that they are fun to write. The most laborious and frustrating part of writing, at least for me, is the struggle to present thoughts in a clear, logical, tonally appropriate, and grammatical way. Theorists are right to call such writing artificial; the words that you are reading now did not arrive as they are printed here. But the human brain processes information most efficiently, and enters the waking dream most easily, when information comes in a clear, coherent, logical way. With no need to wrestle words into their most-digestible form, Difficult poems become, in that regard, easier to write than Less Difficult ones.

It's also easier, when writing Difficult poetry, to follow Pound's commandment: "Make it new." When you can juxtapose anything with

---

309 Burt, *Close Calls With Nonsense*, 11.

anything—and enlist randomness if you need help—newness is readily achieved.

Difficult poems are easier psychologically, too, in that they shield the poet's psyche. T. S. Eliot can't have failed to feel exposed by "The Love Song of J. Alfred Prufrock." *The Waste Land* gave him room to hide.

Irony—a favorite Elliptical tactic—protects the poet's psyche, too. Piled high, irony becomes a wall to hide behind and take potshots. If anyone objects, the Ironist can say, "I didn't mean that. That was irony."

A well-crafted Difficult poem may easily disguise banality. Criticism of Difficult poems necessitates co-creation: impressionistic and highly subjective.

As general readers of poetry fall away, an increasing percentage of the readers who remain are scholars and/or literary experts. These can easily become jaded, in the "Been there, done that" sense, and start leaning toward the esoteric. Yet *they* decide what poetry is taught to novices in classrooms, as well as which poets win awards and are favorably reviewed. Not surprisingly, such readers often prefer Difficult poems, which provide the best chance for experts to "do their thing"—interpret, theorize, lecture, and publish. Difficult poems are a boon to academic careers for those who write them, and for those who write about them, too.

Yet, despite the career advantages of the Difficult, I prefer Less Difficult poems. I reject much of the theory that underpins Difficult writing; and those ideas that seem valid can be addressed without succumbing to Yvor Winters's "fallacy of imitative form"—trying to express disorientation, dislocation, confusion, for instance, with poems that are disorienting, dislocated, and confused. Tony Hoagland, Thomas Lux, Mark Halliday, and others have written entertaining and readable Type A poems that address Type B concerns.

Humor, the ultimate intellectual subversion, allows poets to deal with literary theory—much of which emphasizes subversion of norms—without resorting to Difficult techniques.[310] James Tate, Dean Young, and Lynn Emanuel use humor to express and interrogate the slipperiness of language, shifting and unreliable narrators, fragmentation of experience,

---

310 By humor, I don't mean the willed wackiness of some Difficult poems, which squeeze a superficial strangeness from the conscious mind, trying to impersonate a wild, insouciant intelligence.

lack of closure, moral relativism, indeterminacy, the problem of *meaning*, etc., while keeping at least one foot in Type A territory.

The Fantastic—intense imagination, surrealism, and even absurdism, as in the work of Russell Edson, David Shumate, and Richard Garcia— can also deal cogently and entertainingly with Type B concerns, while giving our brains new and tantalizing stews to chew.

Figurative language has the power to expand the reach of Language in a way that more Difficult techniques approximate, at best. Lyn Hejinian intends, in her prose poems, to make the paragraph "a unit representing a single moment of time, a single moment in the mind, its content all the thought, thought particles, impressions, impulses—all the diverse, particular, and contradictory elements—that are included in an active and emotional mind at any given instant."[311]

She does achieve some interesting effects. But anyone who tries to capture "a single moment" will find that the hand can't write fast enough, even if everything could be simultaneously apprehended, which it can't. Instead, the mind focuses on one item, then another item, and another item, each erasing the "totality" that went before. As Charles Simic states, "Only figurative language can hope to grasp the simultaneity of experience."[312]

The most important reason, though, why I prefer Less Difficult poems is that, even when most brilliant, Difficult poems don't, as a rule, do what I most want poems *to* do: 1. Facilitate the waking dream. 2. Lodge in my memory. 3. Allow me to inhabit—not just ricochet off—fascinating minds. 4. Evoke a wide range of emotions, including positive ones.

Good readers can become almost as involved in a literary situation as in a real one. They laugh and cry, feel fear, anger, desire, elation—experience, in fact, the range of human emotions. Human brains enjoy this state of waking dream, and—led by the Unconscious—move naturally into it. Poetry can encourage this movement by effective use of imagery, rhythm, diction, orchestration, unity, logical development—all the old-fashioned creative writing virtues.

Many characteristics of Difficult poetry—discontinuity, non sequitur, fractured syntax, etc.—disrupt the waking dream, or stop it from happening. The brain reacts, instead, with confusion and anxiety. Rather than re-

---

311 Lyn Hejinian, "The Rejection of Closure," in *Twentieth Century American Poetics*, 369.
312 Charles Simic, "Negative Capability and Its Children," in *Twentieth Century American Poetics*, 369.

lax and let the Unconscious take over, the conscious mind fights to make sense of the disruptive stimuli.

It may be true, as Barthes claims, that by accepting initial befuddlement, ceasing to "resist the ecstatic collapse of cultural assumptions,"[313] a blissful state of *jouissance* can be achieved. But much more commonly, Difficult poetry heightens self-conscious intellectuality.

It also presents a patently false voice. Instead of offering a consciousness that, however unusual, the reader can identify, identify with, and finally, inhabit, Difficult poems may purposely hold readers at bay with a voice that seems autistically distant, schizophrenically fractured, or false in some other way.

In real life—yes, it exists—I dislike people who obfuscate. Nor do I like obfuscating voices in poems. I want to feel that the poem I'm reading arose in someone real who wants intensely to communicate with me. I don't want a speaker who dangles meaning out of reach. Letting me in on the postmodern joke doesn't lessen my annoyance if the speaker wants to show off, more than to connect. The Difficult speaker is often—openly, and by design—a fraud: a Piltdown Man composed of arbitrarily joined parts. Sensing that no such creature ever walked, or could have walked, the earth, I don't enjoy the poem.[314]

In addition to these drawbacks, most (not all!) Difficult poems aren't memorable. Shakespeare's brief candle, Donne's compass, Keats's Grecian urn, Arnold's retreating sea of faith, stay in my mind and change the way I view the world. Among contemporary poems, Kinnell's bear, Komunyakaa's Vietnam Wall, and other images too plentiful to name, have also reshaped my world. Yet, no matter how carefully I read Ashbery, and how impressive his "chops," five minutes later, I've forgotten what I read.

The emotional range of Difficult poetry also seems limited. Poetry has already been shoved onto a small reservation. Difficult poetry further constricts that range, confining the poem mainly to Kafkaesque feelings—confusion, mistrust, anxiety, helplessness, wry humor, despair—or those contemporary favorites: scorn, and knowing self-satisfaction. The strategies of Difficult poetry almost guarantee that these emotions will predominate.

---

313 Selden, Widdowson, and Brooker, *A Reader's Guide to Contemporary Literary Theory*, 158.
314 "If we do not believe the voice in a poem, nothing else matters . . . unless it seems a real voice in a real body in a real world, it is not likely to affect us deeply." David Mason and John Frederick Nims, *Western Wind: An Introduction to Poetry*, 5th ed. (Boston: McGraw Hill, 2006): 7.

Yes, they suit our paranoid and disillusioned time. But do contemporary readers need *poems* to make them anxious and depressed? Or smug?
Shouldn't art help us, at least sometimes, to surmount negative emotions,
rather than intimate that they are all that a moral, intelligent, aware person can legitimately feel?

Conclusion

Everything I've said may be dead wrong. I may be stuck in the past: a dod-
derer preferring tie-dye to Armani, The Beatles and Hendrix to Nicki Mi-
naj and Lil Wayne. But I think the theories behind Difficult poetry are
akin to what adolescents go through when they face their parents' fallibil-
ity, and can't stop barking their outrage. I think the Difficults' methods
limit poetry. I think that they have bet on the wrong horse.

I think this because, though I like some Difficult poems and admire
many, I rarely love reading them. I rarely thrust one at my friends, saying,
"You've got to check this out!"

Maybe I mistake my own habits for Natural Law. Still, I ask more from
poetry than mere intelligence and literary sophistication. I want to spend
my energy resonating with poems, not deciphering them. A poem is not,
for me, holy writ to be pondered endlessly because God's secrets hide inside. I don't mind a little work, but I don't enjoy finishing (co-creating)
incompletely realized poems.

I've heard poets characterize their work as "only as difficult as it has
to be." Do these poets really lug such a weight of brilliance and sensitivity
that only Difficult writing can contain it, and only the most discerning
readers, pick it up? I want to sass back, "Aren't you good enough to make
it clear?"

A quote attributed to Confucius via Ezra Pound states that the whole
of human thought can be entered on the back of a postage stamp. If "human thought" means abstract thought, I agree. Anyway, I don't read poems to increase my stock of abstract thoughts, as Difficult poems encourage me to do. I read to gain vicarious experiences. I read to discover verbal
riches. I read for striking images, startling associations, revelatory metaphors, miracles of wit and imagination. I read to be excited, delighted,
moved—to freshen, deepen, and revitalize my life.

Back in the 1980s, scientists discovered neurons in the human brain
that, when we witness something, fire as if the thing witnessed *is happen-*

ing to us. These "mirror neurons" may explain our powers of empathy, the appeal of narrative, the strength of verbal imagery, the vividness of dreams.

Whether or not mirror neurons are responsible, I want to read poems that feel vivid as life.

As a teacher of poetry workshops, I wonder if I fail my students by not teaching them to write Difficult poems. I worry that Difficult poems may be the natural outcome of a setting in which students and teachers chew and re-chew every poem submitted, searching for a kernel that may not be there.

Good students are, by definition, open and impressionable. Deluged with new ideas, eager for approval, desperate not to seem dense or retrograde, who can blame them for writing to increase coolness and decrease vulnerability? Some workshops instill a loathing of sentimentality and cliché that can spawn a Godzilla-like Poetry Superego, cruel in its defense against "un-problematized" emotions: love, tenderness, joy, grief, rage, enthusiasm. Yet these emotions embody the life-force. They power all of the best art, and—absent religion—are all we have to counter the despair to which rationality, forced to stand alone, must lead.

I don't expect to persuade the already-committed; there's no arguing taste. In any case, just as good psychotherapy depends more on the therapist than the theoretical orientation, every first-rate poet rises above any category to which he or she may be assigned. I don't believe that Poetry will out-popular the Super Bowl if more poets write Less Difficult poems.[315] All the same, I urge the undecided to choose the Less Difficult road, with all its attendant difficulties.

This very week, a famous scholar proclaimed a certain Difficult poet to be, more or less, the new Star in the East. Well, I've seen the star, and won't be following. To write the kind of poems I love to read, poets must be brilliant and skilled enough to communicate without obscurity or obfuscation. They must write, as the best poets always have, with insight, awareness, wit, imagination, passion, intense involvement with life, and all the energy they can muster; and they must do it in the knowledge that general readers—Type A readers like me—are still out there, waiting for poems that speak to them, not just intellect to intellect, but human to human, heart to heart.

---

315 Seeing the fervor with which my son and his friends manipulate their iPads, I fear that reading itself may go the way of cave painting and tossing tree trunks for sport.

Biographical Note

Called "Southern California's most inventive and accessible poet," Charles Harper Webb is also an acclaimed essayist and the nation's foremost proponent of Stand Up Poetry. He has published eleven collections of poems with presses including the University of Wisconsin Press, the University of Pittsburgh Press, and Red Hen Press, as well as a novel with Chatto & Windus (U.K). He has spent his career as a poet and teacher championing reader-friendly poetry, and combating the forces which have driven readers away and consigned the erstwhile Queen of the Arts to the small corner of the cultural basement where she languishes today. Editor of *Stand Up Poetry: An Expanded Anthology*, his awards include the Morse Prize, the Pollock Prize, the Benjamin Saltman Prize, the Kate Tufts Discovery Award, a Whiting Writer's Award, and a Guggenheim fellowship. A licensed psychotherapist and now Professor of English at California State University, Long Beach, he worked for over a decade as a professional rock singer/guitarist.

Printed in the USA
CPSIA information can be obtained
at www.ICGtesting.com
JSHW02233514140824
68134JS00019B/1500